LESSONS IN
LEADERSHIP

D1424270

"John Adair takes us on an evocative journey from the origins of leadership thought ... to reflections on practical wisdom and judgment. In doing so, he achieves his humble aim of sowing within us the seeds of inspiration."

PHIL JAMES, Chief Executive, The Institute of
Leadership & Management

"Leadership expert John Adair packs a lifetime of leadership lessons learned into this fascinating book, chock full of insights and brilliant in its illustrations from both Western and Eastern thought."

CYNTHIA CHERREY, President and CEO,
International Leadership Association

"John Adair's smart, slender volume, *Lessons in Leadership*, summarizes what he has learned over a lifetime of studying and teaching leadership – as well as practising it. Adair's personal and professional trajectory explains why this coda is wise as well as informed."

BARBARA KELLERMAN, James MacGregor Burns Lecturer in
Leadership, Kennedy School, Harvard University

"The author ... explores the journey to becoming an effective strategic leader of an organization. *Lessons in Leadership* is a very inspiring read for anyone who is in a leadership position and wants to better understand their role and thus become more effective."

JOHN FAIRHURST, Managing Director and Academic Principal,
London School of Business and Management

LESSONS IN LEADERSHIP

The 12 Key Concepts

JOHN ADAIR

BLOOMSBURY BUSINESS

LONDON • NEW YORK • OXFORD • NEW DELHI • SYDNEY

BLOOMSBURY BUSINESS
Bloomsbury Publishing Plc
50 Bedford Square, London, WC1B 3DP, UK
1385 Broadway, New York, NY 10018, USA

BLOOMSBURY, BLOOMSBURY BUSINESS and the Diana logo
are trademarks of Bloomsbury Publishing Plc

First published in Great Britain 2018

Copyright © John Adair, 2018

John Adair has asserted his right under the Copyright, Designs and
Patents Act, 1988, to be identified as Author of this work.

Cover design by Emma J. Hardy
Fish icon © Andy Mc / TheNounProject.com

All rights reserved. No part of this publication may be reproduced or
transmitted in any form or by any means, electronic or mechanical, including
photocopying, recording, or any information storage or retrieval system,
without prior permission in writing from the publishers.

Bloomsbury Publishing Plc does not have any control over, or responsibility for,
any third-party websites referred to or in this book. All internet addresses given
in this book were correct at the time of going to press. The author and publisher regret
any inconvenience caused if addresses have changed or sites have
ceased to exist, but can accept no responsibility for any such changes.

A catalogue record for this book is available from the British Library.

Library of Congress Cataloging-in-Publication Data
Names: Adair, John Eric, 1934- author.
Title: Lessons in leadership: the 12 key concepts / John Adair.
Description: New York: Bloomsbury Publishing Plc, [2018] | Includes
bibliographical references and index.
Identifiers: LCCN 2018014204 (print) | LCCN 2018016055 (ebook) | ISBN
9781472956941 (ePub) | ISBN 9781472956927 (ePDF) | ISBN 9781472956958
(eXML) | ISBN 9781472956934 (pbk.: alk. paper)
Subjects: LCSH: Leadership.
Classification: LCC HD57.7 (ebook) | LCC HD57.7 .A27546 2018 (print) | DDC
658.4/092–dc23
LC record available at https://lccn.loc.gov/2018014204

ISBN: PB: 978-1-4729-5693-4
ePDF: 978-1-4729-5692-7
eBook: 978-1-4729-5694-1

Typeset by Deanta Global Publishing Services, Chennai, India
Printed and bound in Great Britain

To find out more about our authors and books visit www.bloomsbury.com and
sign up for our newsletters.

CONTENTS

Introduction

In our complex and interdependent world, vulnerable to
disruption, few things are more important than the quality
and credibility of leaders.

IT IS DIFFICULT to deny the truth of these words. Look at the
news on a television or mobile device, or read today's newspaper,
and what do you find? That our world has indeed a deep and
pressing need for 'good leaders and leaders for good' – in all
fields of human enterprise and at all levels.

On a personal note, may I add that all of my professional life
has been governed by a sense of that need and a determination
to respond to it. In 1979, for example, I became the first person
in the world to hold a university appointment as Professor of
Leadership Studies. More recently, I have served as Chair of
Leadership in the United Nations, based on the UN System Staff
College in Turin.

Since that time, of course, there has been a proliferation of
both courses and professors of leadership in business schools and
universities throughout the world, but especially in America. For

those of us who have been given the rank and title of professor, it is salutary to bear in mind this comment of Einstein: 'Academic chairs are many, but wise and noble teachers are few.'

For the benefit of practical leaders in senior positions, as well as academics, this book is a summary of the main lessons that I have learnt so far about effective leadership. You may be familiar with some of the contents already, notably the chapters relating to Action Centred Leadership, which has been written about extensively and tends to be widely known. Other chapters, however, are much more tentative and exploratory. If you feel that I have left out something of importance, or for that matter included something which belongs elsewhere than under the canopy of leadership, please don't hesitate to let me know: For what matters to all of us in this field is truth.

In fact I do have a very firm belief in the importance of truth. To my mind 'the quality and credibility of leaders' depends ultimately upon whether or not they know and understand the truth about leadership and are willing to live it out whatever the cost – 'truth through personality'.

My own personal quest for the truth about leadership began at a relatively young age. Therefore that story – and in effect the story of this book – starts long ago at St Paul's School in London, way back in 1952, the year when Queen Elizabeth II ascended the throne. I was eighteen years old and came to the subject with a fresh mind and an eagerness to become a good leader myself.

1

First thoughts

Leaders are born not made.
ENGLISH PROVERB

WHILE AT ST PAUL'S SCHOOL I founded the History Society, which, I am pleased to say, survives to this day. In my last term, as its retiring president, I was required to deliver a lecture. I chose as my subject 'leadership in history'. No notes of my lecture survive, but this brief report appeared in the school magazine:

Leadership, he said, could be defined as the activity of influencing people to pursue a certain course; there must also be some power of mind behind the leader. Leadership is not merely the authority of the commander, but contains by necessity some strange strength of personality which attracts the ordinary man. It is only when the times are favourable that a man of destiny can come into his own. Although leadership may change in its aspect from age to age, the qualities of a leader are the same.

Short though it is, this paragraph also has the merit of just about summing up all that was known – or perhaps I should say *believed* – about leadership in those days, namely the mid-twentieth century.

For example, it reflects the assumption in those days that leadership was *male*. Present also at that time are two other assumptions: namely that leadership was both *Western* and essentially *military*.

The alumni of St Paul's School includes not only John Milton and Samuel Pepys but also the great eighteenth-century military commander the Duke of Marlborough, and in modern times Field Marshal Lord Montgomery. In fact, during the Second World War, Montgomery commandeered the large Victorian red-brick building of his old school in Hammersmith to serve as his headquarters for the planning of Operation Overlord in 1944. When he spoke to us schoolboys about his campaigns – in the same lecture theatre which he used to brief General Eisenhower and King George VI on the D-Day landings – 'Monty' on the stage, speaking without notes, personified for me the definitive military leader.

The assumption then, I think it is true to say, was that leadership was something that occurred in *primarily* the military domain, and it was for others to learn from the practice of it on the battlefield.

Therefore, the individuals who could speak with authority on the subject, or so the belief went, were active or retired military officers of distinction. Colonel Lyndon Urwick, a veteran of the trenches, had pioneered that role after the First World War, but as a lone voice. (On a later occasion, he kindly met me for lunch and gave me signed copies of all his relevant books and booklets.)

After the Second World War, Britain's two most successful military leaders – Montgomery and Field Marshal Lord Slim – followed suit. Slim lectured and broadcast widely on leadership; Montgomery less so, although he did write a whole book on the subject entitled *The Path to Leadership* (1961). This was followed by *The Art of Leadership* (1964), a thoughtful book on the traditions of the Royal Navy, written by Captain Stephen Roskill, RN, a distinguished Second World War commander and naval historian, having been given fellowships at a Cambridge college in order to do so.

However, the seepage of leadership from the military domain into the world of work at large does raise two major questions. The first one concerns what is technically called 'transfer'. What grounds have we for believing that the kind of leadership displayed on the battlefield – be it on land, at sea or in the air – is transferable to any kind of peacetime situation?

A rider to this question stems from the fact that in military contexts – as I hinted in my lecture – leadership is inextricably mixed up with command. And so, we must further ask – how far is 'command and control' on the military model relevant to peace situations? Are not war and peace two completely different worlds?

The second question concerns development. Leadership may be a phenomenon that appears in the military domain, but what grounds do we have to believe that it can be developed? The general consensus of military writers in the mid-twentieth century seemed to point in the opposite direction.

LEADERS ARE BORN NOT MADE

AIR VICE MARSHAL 'JOHNNY' JOHNSON was the top British Fighter Command pilot in the Second World War. In his biography *Wing Leader* (1956), Johnson recalls his sense of loss when the legendary Group Captain Douglas Bader was shot down over France.

At Tangmere we had simply judged Bader on his ability as a leader and a fighter pilot, and for us the high sky would never be the same again. Gone was the confident, eager, often scornful voice. Exhorting us, sometimes cursing us, but always holding us together in the fight. Gone was the greatest tactician of them all. Today marked the end of an era that was rapidly becoming a legend.

The elusive, intangible qualities of leadership can never be taught, for a man either has them or he hasn't. Bader had them in full measure and on every flight had shown us how to apply them. He had taught us the true meaning of courage, spirit, determination, guts – call it what you will. Now that he was gone, it was our task to follow his signposts which pointed the way ahead (italics author's).

That English proverb – *Leaders are born not made* – is in fact a very distant descendant of an original Roman proverb, *Nascimur poetae firmus oratores* ('We are born poets, we are made orators'). Down the centuries it came to be applied to other callings, and eventually to leaders.

'Born', in this context, means having from birth – or *as if* from birth – certain specified qualities, such as in this case the quality of leadership. A natural leader – according to this assumption – acts, behaves or operates in accordance with their inherent or innate character.

Proverbs demand brevity, so by their nature tend to oversimplify. You may have noticed the element of *either/or* thinking – black *or* white, born *or* made – has crept into the picture. It is also there in Air Vice Marshal Johnson's statement above, namely that when it comes to the mysterious qualities of leadership, 'a man either has them or he hasn't'. You can see how an assumption of this kind can knock the ground from under any attempt at training for leadership.

In fact we know to the contrary that all natural aptitudes or abilities are arranged on a continuum: Between black and white, there are infinite shades of grey. If you take music, for example, it is clear that natural musicality varies on a scale – ask any choir master. But all musicians – from the truly gifted to those of us with more modest musical abilities – need a strong work motivation in order to develop their talent. Even a Mozart has to practise on the keyboard. In music – as in leadership – the principle is not either/or but both/and. Musicians are both born *and* made.

The legendary cellist Pablo Casals was asked at the age of ninety-two why he still practised for four hours every day. He smiled and replied, 'Because I believe I'm still making progress.'

With leadership, as with love, there does have to be a vital spark. In both cases it is almost impossible to define. *Vital* suggests to me that it is essential to the existence of a thing or to the matter in hand. *Spark*, on the other hand, indicates a particle of a quality, as in 'a spark of interest' or 'a spark of life'. A spark is a latent particle capable of growth and development. Great teachers, incidentally, often live in our minds long after their lessons are forgotten because in some mysterious way they ignited that vital spark of interest in us.

In *The Path to Leadership* (1960), Montgomery made it clear that leadership could be developed:

Some will say that leaders are born, not made, and that you can't make a leader by teaching, or training. I don't agree with this entirely. While it is true that some men have within themselves the instincts and qualities of leadership in a much great degree than others, and some men will never have the character to make leaders, I believe that leadership can be developed by training. In the military sphere, I reckon that soldiers will be more likely to follow a leader in whose military knowledge they have confidence, rather than a man with much greater personality but with not the same obvious knowledge of his job. ... I know I found this to be the case myself in 1914, when as a young lieutenant I commanded a platoon and had to lead them in charges against entrenched Germans, or undertake patrol activities in no-man's land. By the training I had received from my superiors in peacetime, I gained confidence in my ability to deal with any situation likely to confront a young officer of my rank in war; this increased my morale and my powers of leading my platoon, and later my company.

By leadership training, Montgomery seems to be talking about the acquisition of a commanding 'military knowledge'. But when my book *Training for Leadership* appeared in 1968, charting the introduction of the Three-Circles model at Sandhurst as a much wider basis for leadership development, he kindly read it 'with the greatest of interest' and characteristically added in his handwritten letter to me: 'Leadership is an immense subject ... nowhere is it more important to teach it than at Sandhurst and in our universities; in fact, to youth, since it falls on dead ground with the older generation.'

* * * * * * *

So far I have been discussing the military as the reputed home of leadership from the outside. But in 1952 all young men were required to do two years of military conscription, still known in Winston Churchill's brilliant wartime phrase as *National Service*. As it happened, Paul, my elder brother, had left St Paul's School and gone to Sandhurst, from where he had been recently commissioned into the Coldstream Guards. So in 1953 I followed in his footsteps and presented myself at the Guards Depot in Caterham for the required weeks of basic training.

Not long afterwards I experienced for myself one excellent legacy from the Second World War: the War Office Selection Board. In *Great Leaders* (1989) I gave this brief account of the method:

> In the first year of the war, the British Army relied upon the interview for choosing officers. Questions of the type, 'What school did you go to?' and 'What does your father do?' were customary. Such interviews, conducted by amateurs, were poor tools for predicting leadership performance. Twenty-five per cent (and in one case fifty per cent) of those picked out by these methods were subsequently returned to their units from the officer training schools as being unfit to lead platoons.
>
> Alarmed by the high rate of failure and its effects on the individuals concerned, the Adjutant-General of the day, Sir

Ronald Adam, assembled a working party of senior officers and psychologists, including an American called W.R. Bion, who later made a distinguished contribution in the field of social psychology. Together they developed a new method of selecting leaders, called the War Office Selection Board (WOSB). It was the grandfather of all the assessment centres we know today.

A WOSB was spread over several days. It was based on the principle of selecting leaders for groups by placing candidates in groups, and giving each group some specific tasks to perform. The tasks were developed to include outdoor exercises, such as getting a barrel over a stream with limited equipment. Various aptitude tests, role plays, presentations, group leadership tests and an assault course were all fitted into three days. The pace and demands of the programme introduced an element of stress: no bad thing when one is selecting leaders for battle. The selectors then watched the 'command tasks' with particular attention, to see how far each candidate performed the necessary functions to help the group to achieve its task and to hold the team together as a working unit. In other words, the working group used an embryo form of the three-circles approach, together with the concept of functions that would meet these needs. This was a very different concept from that which assumed a leader was born with certain leadership qualities, such as patience and determination, which would equip him or her to lead in any situation.

At Infantry Officer Training Unit, apart from being given a single sheet of paper containing a list of the seventeen 'Qualities required in a leader', there was no further instruction in leadership on offer.

Having been commissioned into the Scots Guards in 1953, I joined the 1st Battalion then in camp just south of Port Said in Egypt. The following year I became the only National Service officer to serve in the Arab Legion, as the Jordanian Army was then known. There I found myself in its newly raised 9th Regiment, which consisted of some 900 Bedouin soldiers recruited from northern and central Arabia. The regiment was deployed around the Old City of Jerusalem – then still in Jordanian hands – and had its headquarters on the Mount of Olives, where I had a room on the eastern slope, looking out over the wilderness of Judea to the Dead Sea and the blue mountains of Moab in the distance. Colonel Peter Young, the only other British officer in the regiment, surprised both me and his superiors by making me the adjutant of the regiment. On the first evening of my arrival, a Bedouin officer of the Bani Howeitat gave me one of his tribe's traditional names – Sweillim – and thereafter that was how I was known to all.

By this time in my mind I had simplified leadership down into just one principle: *Leadership is example.* It seemed to sum up all that we knew.

One influence upon me to think in this way was Lawrence of Arabia, whom I had studied since I was a boy. 'The Bedouin are difficult to drive, but easy to lead,' wrote Lawrence. He added: 'They taught me that no man could be their leader except he ate the rank's food, wore their clothes, lived level with them, and yet appeared better in himself.'

Outside Jerusalem one morning I met for the first time the legendary commander-in-chief of the Arab Legion, Glubb Pasha. As I walked beside him on a tour of our defensive works, he asked me about myself, and then added, 'It is rather fun here, isn't it?'

Much later in life Glubb Pasha's casual words would come back to me. For I read in them a lesson about leadership. By fun, I believe he meant an activity that engages one's interest and imagination, even if it is one that could involve some very hard work. Glubb was sharing with me what he still experienced after a life time spent in military service with the Bedouin army.

Like Lawrence of Arabia, Glubb led by example. Several years later, after we had become friends, I asked him about leadership. In his letter of reply, dated 12 June 1984, he stressed the importance of example:

> Your subject of leadership is a fascinating one. In desert police posts in Jordan, I had a notice posted in every fort – 'Example is stronger than advice, so guide the people by your own noble deeds.'

Could one say that '*do it yourself*' is a good motto for leaders?

I once received indirectly a tribute which gave me great pleasure. It was written by one of my former soldiers to a third party, who sent it on to me. It said (of myself), 'He never asked his men to do anything he did not do himself.'

In Jordan, a great part of the desert was strewn with boulders of lava from ancient extinct volcanoes. A local nomadic tribe called 'Ahl al jebel', the mountain people, lived in the lava fields. They made a practice in the evening of suddenly sallying forth from the lava, rounding up half a dozen camels or sheep from a tribe camped in the gravelly desert, and dashing back into the lava. I had a desert patrol of Bedouins in Ford trucks, who kept order in the open desert, but our trucks, it was thought, could not operate in the lava.

One day with a patrol of ten men in two trucks I drove up to the edge of the lava and started clearing lava blocks out of the way. Bedouins in those early days fancied themselves as warriors, but despised people who *worked*, like fellaheen! They would have been indignant if anyone had suggested that they should work as labourers.

So I got out of my car and started lifting rocks. Within a minute, all the men were with me lifting rocks, without me saying a word. We got a track several yards long into the lava that day, and within a week or two we had cleared so far into the lava that the tribal shaikhs realized that their isolation was at an end, and came to call on us and drink coffee, and ask what the government had ordered.

If I had first paraded my men and told them we were going to clear tracks through the lava, they would not have been at all pleased! So 'do it yourself' was indeed the secret of success in that particular instance.

* * * * * * *

As my months living on the eastern edge of the Mount of Olives drew to their close, my thoughts turned to my future career. My provisional intention was to become a leader in Britain's deep-sea fishing industry, based then in Hull and Grimsby. The principle of *leadership is example* required me to prove that I could lead fishermen, not just manage the business from an office desk, and to do that I had to become one of them.

Therefore, on the day after my National Service ended, I took the train to Hull. After qualifying to be a deckhand at Hull Nautical College, I joined the crew of the *Camilla*, a steam trawler fishing off Iceland. For a month, except when sailing between fishing grounds, I worked my watch every three hours, gutting the trawl and stacking it on ice below. It was off Iceland that I learnt that the longing for sleep can surpass any other longing!

The wintry conditions at sea that winter north of Iceland were appalling. The trawlers became encased with ice and frozen snow; two of them in our vicinity capsized and sank with the loss of fifty lives. At least I was sharing the dangers and hardships of the men whom one day in the future I hoped to lead.

Even in those conditions, so different from the military world, I witnessed the power of example, of leading from the front.

Ask not of others

At the age of twenty, as I have mentioned, I was working as a deckhand on a Hull fishing trawler. The mate in charge of the deckhands was a large bully of a man with a chip on his shoulder, for he had recently been a skipper but lost his ticket through incompetence.

One afternoon, in a winter storm near Iceland, he told one of the men to shin up the mast and adjust an unsafe navigation light. 'Not bloody likely', said the man, looking at the kicking mast and hissing waves. 'You do it, Bill', thundered the mate to another deckhand. 'Not me', replied Bill with a shrug. The mate began to shout and swear at us all.

Attracted by the commotion on deck, the skipper came down from the bridge. 'What's up?' he asked. The mate told him. 'Why don't you go up yourself?' the skipper said to the mate, looking him in the eye. Silence. 'Right, I'll do it myself', said the skipper, and began to pull off his oilskin. He meant it too. At once three or four men stepped forward and volunteered for we had no desire to lose our navigator overboard.

Which was the true leader – the mate or the skipper?

2

Leading from the front

*Not the cry but the flight of the wild duck leads the flock
to fly and to follow.*
CHINESE PROVERB

'PAINTING A PICTURE or writing a book', said the great artist
Henri Matisse, is 'always best done if I move from the simple to
the complex'. The focus of this book is upon what leaders *do*:
the action-centred leadership approach. Now if we take seriously
the dictum that *leadership is done from in front*, it is that simple
action which is our starting point. So let us try to understand
that first and then explore the more complex aspects later.

Why do leaders go first in this manner? The common answer
is that they do so in order to show the way, or – in other words
– to ensure that those following behind them are going in the
right direction. But a moment's thought tells us that soldiers on a
battlefield know in what direction they have to march or run to
engage their enemy. And in wider contexts, showing the way is

the function of a *guide* on land and a *pilot* at sea. As there are no exact synonyms in the English language we must look elsewhere to discover what function a leader – as opposed to a guide or pilot – is performing when he leads from the front. Oddly enough, the clue lies buried in the etymology of the verb 'to lead'.

The word 'leadership' itself didn't enter the English language until the 1820s. The three constituent elements, however, that make up the composite word – LEAD.ER.SHIP – all date back to Old English, the language of the Angles and Saxons, and its kindred North European languages. That is why today you will find the English word 'leader' in, for example, German (leiter), Dutch (leider) and Norwegian (leder).

* * * * * * *

The first element in leadership – LEAD – means a way, path, track or the course of a ship at sea. It is a journey word. In its simple verbal form, to *lead* meant 'to go' or 'to travel'. But in Old English that direct form of the verb is missing. What we have is only the *causative* form of the verb. So to lead (*lædan*) in English uniquely means to *cause* someone or something to move forward or to go on a journey.

How do you cause people – people who are both free and equal – to advance in this way? By the simple act of leading them from the front. Or, as Glubb Pasha put it in the last chapter, 'Do it yourself.'

But why does it work? To find the answer – or at least pick up a clue – we must turn to the natural world. In the regions around the Mediterranean, the picture of a shepherd leading his flock of sheep from the front to pasture is still a common sight. For it is a fact that sheep are relatively easy to lead from the front but are difficult to drive forward without scattering them from the rear. Shepherds in northern Greece today, like their ancient counterparts, have mastiffs to help them guard their flocks against wolves. Sheepdogs, however, which are bred and trained to round up sheep and drive them from the rear upon signals from the shepherd, are a relatively modern phenomenon.

The same causative effect, we may surmise, has been observed among people. When one tribal warrior went ahead first, others would follow. If he did it more than once, he would become known as a lead-er (for the –er suffix indicates someone who does something more than once, as in carpenter or dancer).

When nation states began to form in the Near East, some of these warrior-leaders were chosen – or put themselves forward – to be kings. Saul in the land occupied by the twelve Hebrew tribes is one example, and the kings chosen by the Spartans another. The prime and most simple function of such kings was to lead the nation's army into battle – from the front.

In fact, the earliest example of writing known to history – some words engraved on a Sumerian pottery shard found near Babylon and dated to about 4,500 BCE – makes a direct link between the causative function of a shepherd and that of a king. It is in the form of a proverb: *Soldiers without a king are like sheep without a shepherd.*

Beyond that proverb, it is fair to say that the ancient civilizations around the Mediterranean are silent on the subject of leadership. There is, however, one great exception: Athens in the age of Socrates (469–399 BCE).

* * * * * * *

The ancient Greeks were a warrior people by origin. Homer, their great poet of the eighth century BCE, expressed the heroic Greek spirit in the *Iliad*, his epic poem of the long war against Troy:

All dreadful glared the iron face of war,
But touched with joy the bosoms of the brave.

Even in the cultural heyday of Athens in the fifth century BCE, the Greek cities spent an inordinate amount of time fighting each other or at war with their common enemy, the neighbouring Great Persian Empire. Socrates himself took part in three campaigns as a hoplite, as the heavily armed foot soldiers were called. Usually, hoplites fought in a phalanx, a compact body of soldiers drawn up in close order for battle.

Xenophon (pronounced in English as Zenophon), the son of Gryllus, a member of an aristocratic and comparatively wealthy family, secured election as a cavalry commander at a young age. In 401 BCE, contrary to the advice of Socrates, he joined an army of Greek mercenaries hired by a Persian prince, Cyrus the Younger.

The real reason for their service the Greek army – known to history as the 'Ten Thousand' – only discovered when they arrived in the vicinity of Babylon: It was to enable Cyrus to seize the Persian throne. But although his Greek mercenaries fought valiantly in a decisive battle with the incumbent (who also had a Greek contingent in his army), Cyrus lost both the battle and his life.

Faced now with a stark choice of death or slavery, the Greek officers – as if by common consent by the more senior of their six generals, a Spartan called Clearchus – directed their army to march 900 miles north through enemy country to the Black Sea and freedom. Not long after they set out on this epic march, the Persians invited the six Greek generals to a parley – and after the final course of the feast, put them all to the sword. Now the advantage of democracy showed itself, for the remaining Greek officers, far from scattering like frightened sheep, assembled together and elected six generals to take their place. Xenophon, then aged about twenty-six years, was one of the chosen six. The *Anabasis* (literally the 'going up') is Xenophon's account of the expedition and its return to safety. Incidentally, T. E. Lawrence modelled *The Seven Pillars of Wisdom*, his epic account of the Arab Revolt in the First World War, on the *Anabasis*. Like Xenophon, he magnified his own role into that of being in effect the commandeer-in-chief. In neither man was modesty a strong point.

Imagine yourself on a sun-baked, stony hillside on the southern edge of Kurdistan (on the borders of what is now Iraq and Turkey) watching this scene unfold before you: it is about noon; the sky is clear blue, except for a line of white clouds almost motionless above a distant mountain range. Marching through these foothills comes the advance guard of the Ten Thousand. The hot sun glints and sparkles on their spears, helmets and breastplates. They are hurrying forward, eager to reach the safety of the mountains in order to be rid of the Persian cavalry snapping at their heels. But first they have to cut their way through the Carduci, the warrior tribe of the region. Across the pass you can see a strong contingent of these tribesmen already occupying the lower heights of a steep hill which commands the road. Now the Greek advance guard spotted them, too, and it halts. After some hurried deliberations you can see a messenger running back. A few minutes later a horseman – it is Xenophon – gallops up to the commander of the advance guard, a seasoned Spartan captain named Chirisophus. Xenophon tells him that he has not brought up a reinforcement of the light-armed troops that had been urgently requested because the rearguard – still under constant attack – could not be weakened. Then he carefully studies the lie of the land. Noticing that the Carduci have neglected to occupy the actual summit of the hill, he puts this plan to his Spartan colleague:

> The best thing to do, Chirisophus, is for us to advance on the summit as fast as we can. If we can occupy it, those who are commanding our road will not be able to maintain their position. If you like, you stay here with the main body. I will volunteer to go ahead. Or, if you prefer it, you march on the mountain and I will stay here.
>
> 'I will give you the choice', replies Chirisophus 'of doing whichever you like.'

It would be an arduous physical task, Xenophon pointed out, and he tactfully says that being the younger man, he would be the best one to undertake it. Having chosen some 400 skirmishers, armed with targets and light javelins, together with 100 hand-picked hoplites of the advance guard, he marched them off as fast as he could go towards the summit. But when the enemy see what the Greeks are doing, they too begin to head for the highest ground as fast as they can go.

> Then there was a lot of shouting, from the Greek army cheering on its men on the one side and from Tissaphernes' people cheering on their men on the other side. Xenophon rode along the ranks on horseback, urging them on. 'Soldiers', he said, 'consider that it is for Greece you are fighting now,

that you are fighting your way to your children and your wives, and that with a little hard work now, we shall go on the rest of our way unopposed'.

Soteridas, a man from Sicyion, said: 'We are not on a level, Xenophon. You are riding on horseback, while I am wearing myself out with a shield to carry.'

As the commander, Xenophon had several options open to him. He could have ignored the man. Or he could have threatened him. Or he could conceivably have had him arrested and punished later. Xenophon took none of these courses. Writing of himself in the third person, he told us what happened next:

When Xenophon heard this, he jumped down from his horse, pushed Soteridas out of the ranks, took his shield away from him and went forward on foot as fast as he could, carrying the shield. He happened to be wearing a cavalry breastplate as well, so that it was heavy going for him. He kept on encouraging those in front to keep going and those behind to join up with them, though struggling along behind them himself. The other soldiers, however, struck Soteridas and threw stones at him and cursed him until they forced him to take back his shield and continue marching. Xenophon then remounted and, so long as the going was good, led the way on horseback. When it became impossible to ride, he left his horse behind and hurried ahead on foot. And so they got to the summit before the enemy.

Note that it was the other soldiers who shamed Soteridas into taking back his shield. Although Xenophon, burdened with a heavy cavalry breastplate, eventually fell back behind the ranks as the men rushed up the hill, yet he encouraged the men forward and urged them to keep their battle order. Eventually, he remounted and led his soldiers from the front, at first on horse and then again on foot.

Once the Greeks had gained the summit the Carduci turned and fled in all directions. The Persian cavalry under Tissaphernes, who had been distant onlookers of the contest, also turned their bridles and withdrew. Eventually, in the summer of the following year, the army reached the safety of the Hellespont, the narrow straits dividing Europe from Asia. They owed much to Xenophon who, not long afterwards, became the sole commander of the Ten Thousand.

Xenophon seems to have learnt a lesson from the skirmish with the Carduci. Later, when leading his men to attack an enemy in Thrace, he dismounted, explaining to a surprised fellow officer that 'the hoplites will run faster and more cheerfully if I lead on foot'.

* * * * * * *

If we fast forward to the history of England, we find the same phenomenon: It is the act of leading from in front which causes men to follow a leader, voluntarily and as if of their own free will. The movement caused by command from above or from the rear, backed as it may be by the threat of a draconian punishment for disobedience, simply lacks the same magic power.

Towards the end of Shakespeare's play *Macbeth*, the generals still loyal to the 'confident tyrant' are discussing their master's total lack of leadership. The most dangerous consequence one of them, Angus, declares is that in battle

> *His army moves only by command,*
> *Nothing by love.*

Therefore, Angus in effect concludes, the coming final battle to secure his ill-gotten throne is already lost.

By contrast, in *Henry V*, Shakespeare portrays an ideal leader – one with all the 'king-becoming graces' – who leads his army from in front to great victory at Agincourt.

Incidentally, Shakespeare puts into King Henry's mouth some long and inspiring speeches before the siege of Harfleur – 'Once more unto the breach dear friends, once more' – and again before Agincourt: 'We few, we happy few, we band of brothers.' But, according to a contemporary chronicler – very possibly an eye witness – what Henry actually says as he led his men forwards towards the much larger French army is 'Come on, fellas'. True leaders are always strong on action and usually very economical with words. But then they don't have a theatre to fill!

* * * * * * *

What is now clear is the truth of Euripides' verse: 'Ten soldiers wisely led will beat a hundred without a head.' Therefore wise armies foster a culture where officers are expected by their soldiers to lead them from in front, and officers can have complete trust that if they do so, the men will follow them.

By the eighteenth century the English standing army, the Redcoats, exhibited that unwritten contract – one of mutual expectations, as if between equals – between officers and the rank and file. In an article entitled 'The Bravery of the English Soldier', which appeared in a monthly journal called *The Idler* in 1760, Dr Samuel Johnson reflected upon this unseen but very real contract:

> By those who have compared the military genius of the English with that of the French nation, it is remarked that 'the French officers will always lead, if the soldiers will follow'; and that 'the English soldiers will always follow, if their officers will lead'.

> In all pointed sentences some degrees of accuracy must be sacrificed to conciseness; and, in this comparison, our officers seem to lose what our soldiers gain. I know not any reason for

supposing that the English officers are less willing than the French to lead; but it is, I think, universally allowed, that the English soldiers are more willing to follow.

Our nation may boast, beyond any other people in the world, of a kind of epidemic bravery, diffused equally through all its ranks. We can show a peasantry of heroes, and fill our armies with clowns, whose courage may vie with that of their general.

On occasion English soldiers could be quite outspoken to officers whom they suspected to be shirking their role of leading from the front. One soldier in Wellington's army during the Peninsular War, for example, writes in his memoir, 'Our men had divided the officers into classes – the "Come on" and the "Go on"', for as Tom Plunkett in action once observed to an officer, 'The words "Go on" don't befit a leader, Sir'. Plunkett was absolutely right.

Both on land and at sea, soldiers and sailors – as their memoirs often reveal – scrutinized their officers very thoroughly, both in terms of their professional knowledge and experience and with regard to their leadership qualities. This kind of upwards scrutiny, of course, is not confined to the armed services. Even at school, if you remember, you knew within days exactly how far you could go with a given teacher.

* * * * * * *

To lead soldiers from the front to make a highly dangerous and risky journey, often towards a waiting enemy, may be causative but it may also be a death sentence for the leader. The reason why this should be the case is indicated by a proverb that Jesus is said to have quoted (Matthew 26:31): *Strike the shepherd and the sheep of the flock will scatter*. If an enemy force is advancing towards you it is instinctive to shoot the leaders – those out in front – first: not just because they are the first to come into range but because by downing them it may cause the followers to waiver, lose their order and turn to run away.

Even in ancient times, leading from the front was extremely life-threatening. Research shows that no leader of a Greek phalanx on the losing side of a battle ever survived. With the introduction of the machine gun in the First World War – there were over ten million of these deadly weapons in service – the death toll of regimental officers was appalling. In the Second World War, when, as chief of the General Staff, Field Marshall Alanbrooke had great difficulty in finding generals who had the necessary qualities of leadership at that level, he blamed it on the First World War. In his private diary he wrote: 'Those that had fallen were the born leaders of men, in command of companies and battalions. It was always the best that fell by taking the lead.'

Even before the end of the First World War, the German Army, and belatedly the British Army, had begun to develop new tactics that did not turn their officers into fodder fire for the machine guns. But such deadly ingrained role expectations are not so easily eradicated. Professor Sir Michael Howard, the eminent military historian, recalls his discovery of this fact while serving as a newly arrived platoon commander in the Coldstream Guards at Salerno during the Second World War. He received a command to take part in a daylight attack on a strongly defended hill, an episode he describes in his autobiography:

> When I gave the leading section its orders, the sergeant in charge asked incredulously 'Aren't you going to lead us, sir?' The look of amazed contempt that he gave me when I said that I was not is something that I shall never forget. The other platoon commanders did lead their platoons. All were killed or badly wounded.

* * * * * * *

On the above (p. 5) I raised a fundamental question: How far is leadership, as exhibited in military contexts, transferable to other domains or fields?

What is clearly not transferable is the specific form of military command; the rationale for that practice is rooted in the unnatural conditions of war. (Although in the English language the term 'commander' was once a close synonym of 'leader', it is now restricted as a role title to the armed forces and to certain uniformed emergency services such as the police.)

If we take *leading from the front* (in the physical or literal sense) as a particular form of *leading by example*, then the door of transferability is wide open, for there are a thousand ways of leading by example. And, incidentally, a thousand ways exist for *not* leading by example! Take pastors as a case in point.

'It is certain', Shakespeare wrote in *Henry IV*, Part Two, 'that either wise bearing or ignorant carriage is caught, as men take diseases, therefore let men take heed of their company'. In the West no less than in the East, or in tribal societies, the power of moral – or immoral – example has always been well understood. In Christendom the failure of spiritual leaders to lead from in front, by good example, always troubled the best minds. As Shakespeare put it,

Do not like some ungracious pastors do,
Show us the steep and thorny way to heaven,
While they the primrose path of dalliance tread
And reck [follow] not their own rede [advice].

* * * * * * *

'We shall find again and again', writes C. S. Lewis in *Studies in Words* (1960), 'the earliest senses of a word flourishing for centuries, despite a vast overgrowth of later senses which might be expected to kill them'.

Leadership from in front is a case in point. The earliest sense of it is still with us today. Even in the military field, where occasions for literally leading soldiers from in front into battle are now far less common, it is still a very potent phrase. And it serves as a concrete and visual reference point, a kind of hidden anchor beneath all our metaphorical uses of such terms as 'leading', 'leader' and 'leadership'.

* * * * * * *

One archaic survivor, however, of the original metaphor is the word 'follower'. It is a fossil word. For it applied to those who followed a leader on a literal journey, just as sheep follow a shepherd. Remove that literal journey and the term 'follower' has to be treated as a metaphor, nothing more.

Unfortunately, the English language has no clear-cut replacement name to denote those who work in teams with leaders. Therefore, to some extent, we are still saddled with leader–*followers* as a general coupling, comparable to doctors–patients or teachers–students, lawyers–clients, or sellers–buyers. But it carries some of the wrong connotations for today's world. Here are my reasons for that judgment.

In English, 'supporter' is the general term for one who allies himself or herself with a cause or shows allegiance to its leader. 'Follower' and 'disciple' are related because they emphasize devotion to a leader rather than a doctrine or cause. A *follower* plays a more passive role than a *supporter* or a *disciple*. A *disciple* is one who studies under a leader or teacher of great influence and puts the leader's teaching into practice, perhaps to the point of proselytizing for him.

Just to complete the picture, an *adherent* places emphasis on support of the doctrines rather than of the leader himself. So it is that we speak of Lenin as having been an *adherent* of Marxism, not an *adherent* of Marx himself.

Notice that overtone or connotation of passivity in the notion of being a *follower*: the word suggests not much more than imitating the person in front of one, not unlike the children's game *Follow-my-leader*, in which each player must exactly imitate the actions of the leader or pay a forfeit.

Apart from the implied sense of sheep-like passivity, 'follower' also has – at least in modern usage – a potentially more dangerous connotation: for it is the inclusive term for a person who attaches themselves to the person or opinion of another. That attachment may spring from choice or conviction on rational grounds. Equally, however, it may be an unhealthy form of attachment, where a charismatic leader such as Adolf Hitler demands complete loyalty to him personally, right or wrong. Even in cases where malevolent charisma is not involved, some of the synonyms for 'follower', such as 'partisan', 'henchman' or 'satellite', designate a person in whom personal devotion overshadows or eclipses their critical faculties. No true leader demands personal loyalty as of right or at the expense of all other considerations.

In 1928 the term 'followership' made its first appearance in American dictionaries, where it was defined as 'the capacity or willingness to follow a leader'. In recent years there have been attempts to give the term more substance than that, to build it up as a counter-balance, so to speak, to leadership. But because 'follower' is actually an archaic term, these efforts are like trying to inflate an empty balloon. The –*ship* suffix here denotes neither a single generic role (as in leadership) nor a collection of generic skills (as in craftsmanship).

Yet there remains a fundamental truth that proponents of followership are right to emphasize: namely that occupying a subordinate role in a work group or organization doesn't ever strip away or erode one's moral responsibility as a person and as a citizen. If any leader – at any level – oversteps the mark in the moral sense, members of such a body should refuse to follow in their footsteps, and moreover, call them to account, for it is the essence of democracy that, as free and equal people, leaders are ultimately accountable to the people.

For the time being, alas, we simply don't have an inclusive term to connect with 'leader' in the generic role relation, so we shall continue to use 'follower' or 'followers'. To adapt an old proverb, 'There are no bad followers, only bad leaders'. This is true up to a point, but yet isn't it as much true to claim 'There are no bad leaders, only bad followers'?

Montgomery once told me his secret as a leader: 'I made my soldiers partners with me in the battle.' Isn't that what all real leaders aim to do? They want equals, not followers or subordinates, and they see their role as being what the Romans called *primus inter pares*: 'first among equals'. And the devotion they solicit is for a common cause, not for themselves considered as individuals. Banesh Hoffman wrote of his experience as a colleague of Albert Einstein: 'If you worked with him he made you aware of a common enemy – the problem. And you became his partner in battle.'

3

Sharing dangers and hardships

I am among you as one who serves
JESUS OF GALILEE

THE CAUSATIVE NATURE of leading people from the front is, as far as I know, universal. As social beings we are, to a greater or lesser degree, ductile: prone to being led. But that propensity is greatly strengthened if there is respect and liking, though not necessarily love, for the person who is in the role of leader. In other words, the personality or character of a leader, as expressed in their attitudes and behaviour, does have an important part to play in the willingness of others to follow.

Xenophon gives us character sketches of two of the six generals in office when he joined the Ten Thousand in Babylon.

He clearly demonstrates how personal qualities influence the effectiveness of both leadership and command.

Proxenus the Boeotian had invited Xenophon to join him on the Persian expedition, and so they were probably friends. Proxenus was a very ambitious young man and had spent much money on being educated by a celebrated teacher called Gorgias of Leontini. 'After he had been with him for a time', wrote Xenophon, 'he came to the conclusion that he was now capable of commanding an army and, if he became friends with the great, of doing them no less good than they did him; so he joined in this adventure planned by Cyrus, imagining that he would gain from it a great name, and great power, and plenty of money'. Proxenus, however, liked to be liked, which led him – as with many a later leader – into the mistakes of appearing soft and of courting popularity for its own sake:

> He was a good commander for people of a gentlemanly type, but he was not capable of impressing his soldiers with a feeling of respect or fear for him. Indeed, he showed more diffidence in front of his soldiers than his subordinates showed in front of him, and it was obvious that he was more afraid of being unpopular with his troops than his troops were afraid of disobeying his orders. He imagined that to be a good general, and to gain the name for being one, it was enough to give praise to those who did well and to withhold it from those who

did badly. The result was that decent people in his entourage liked him, but unprincipled people undermined his position, since they thought he was easily managed. At the time of his death he was about thirty years old.

By contrast, Clearchus, the veteran (at fifty years old) Spartan general who saved the day after the Battle of Cunaxa, could never be accused of wanting to be liked. Indeed, he seemed to go too far in the opposite direction. As Xenophon noted, Clearchus never won the hearts of men, and had no followers who were there because of friendship or positive feelings towards him. Xenophon continues:

He had an outstanding ability for planning means by which an army could get supplies, and seeing that they appeared; and he was also well able to impress on those who were with him that Clearchus was a man to be obeyed. He achieved this result by his toughness. He had a forbidding appearance and a harsh voice. His punishments were severe ones and were sometimes inflicted in anger, so that there were times when he was sorry himself for what he had done. With him, punishment was a matter of principle, for he thought that an army without discipline was good for nothing; indeed, it is reported that he said that a soldier ought to be more frightened of his own commander than of the enemy if he was going to turn out one who could keep a good guard, or abstain from doing harm to his own side, or go into battle without second thoughts.

So it happened that in difficult positions the soldiers would give him complete confidence and wished for no one better. ... On the other hand, when the danger was over and there was a chance of going away to take service under someone else, many of them deserted him, since he was invariably tough and savage, so that the relations between his soldiers and him were like those of boys to a schoolmaster.

Doubtless Xenophon resolved in his mind to find the golden mean: the middle course of leadership and command between the extremes of Proxenus and Clearchus.

* * * * * * *

What also stands out clearly from Xenophon's writings is that leaders who shared the dangers, hardships and labours of their men are more likely to win their hearts and minds.

Again, we are here in the realm of universal truth: neither ancient nor modern, neither Western nor Eastern. Take this brief account by Hsun Tzu, the Master Hsun, one of the great Confucian philosophers. Writing in about 200 BCE, he gives us this vivid account of what it means for a military leader to share hardships and dangers:

In ancient times good generals were always in the vanguard themselves. They didn't set up canopies in the heat and didn't wear leather in the cold; thus they experienced the same heat and cold as their soldiers.

They did not ride over rough terrain, always dismounting when climbing hills; thus they experienced the same toil as their soldiers.

They would eat only after food had been cooked for the troops, and they would drink only after water had been drawn for the troops; thus they experienced the same hunger and thirst as their soldiers.

In battle they would stand within range of enemy fire; thus they experienced the same dangers as their soldiers.

So in their military operations, good generals always use accumulated gratitude to attack accumulated bitterness. And accumulated love to attack accumulated hatred. Why would they not win?

Those who are near will not hide their ability, and those who are distant will not grumble at their toil. … That is what is called being a leader and teacher of men.

Similarly, the Roman legions valued a general who did not absent himself from their tasks, trials and tribulations. The Greek biographer and philosopher Plutarch, writing in the early second century CE, comments that such a commander won the affection of the soldiers by showing that they could live as hard as they did and endure just as much.

> Indeed it seems generally to be the case that our labours are eased when someone goes out of his way to share them with us; it has the effect of making the labour not seem forced. And what a Roman soldier likes most is to see his general eating his ration of bread with the rest, or sleeping on an ordinary bed, or joining in the work of digging a trench or raising a palisade. The commanders whom they admire are not so much those who distribute honours and riches as those who take a share in their hardships and dangers; they have more affection for those who are willing to join in their work than for those who indulge them in allowing them to be idle.

Apart from his open-handed generosity with the rewards of victory – a trait which British tribal war leaders would recognize – Julius Caesar certainly led by example. There was no danger that he was not willing to face, nor no form of hard work from which he excused himself. Like Alexander, his great exemplar, Caesar had a passion for distinction which enabled him to overcome the disadvantages of a slightly built physique, and a proneness to migraine and epileptic fits. 'Yet so far from making his poor health an excuse for living an easy life', continued Plutarch, 'he used warfare as a tonic for his health. By long hard journeys, simple diet, sleeping night after night in the open, and rough living he fought off his illness and made his body strong enough to stand up to anything'.

Under Caesar's eye the Roman legions became 'an unconquered and unconquerable army'. For Caesar's very presence seemed to transform ordinary professional legionaries into men of extraordinary valour. 'Soldiers who in other campaigns had not shown themselves to be any better than average', wrote Plutarch, 'became irresistible and invincible and ready to confront any danger.'

* * * * * * *

From all these military instances, we can see that a leader who leads by example, who shares in the task in a 'hands on' way, while also directing others and encouraging them by word as well as example, is going to have a positive influence on his soldiers. But does this combination work on civilians? Xenophon leaves us in no doubt.

For when Xenophon was not campaigning, he exercised leadership among the farm labourers on his estate (a gift from the Spartans) and added to his prolific writings. He returned to the theme of leadership in his most influential book, the *Cyropaedia*. In later centuries it became *the* textbook on leadership for many of the great leaders of Rome. As the strange-sounding title suggests, the *Cyropaedia* is a philosophical dialogue about the education of Cyrus the Great, who in fact does little more than lend his name to an ideal king ruling an ideal state.

In it, Xenophon advocated that a leader should demonstrate that in summer he can endure the heat, and in winter the cold; and he should show that in difficult times he can endure the hardships as well as, if not better than, his men. Moreover, a leader should rejoice with them if any good befell them and sympathize with them if any ills overtook them, showing himself eager to help in times of stress. 'It is in these respects that you should somehow go hand-in-hand with them,' wrote Xenophon. 'All this contributes to the leader being loved by his men.' Xenophon added the interesting observation that it was actually easier for the leader to endure heat and cold, hunger and thirst, want and hardship, than his followers. 'The general's position, and the very consciousness that nothing he does escapes notice, lightens the burden for him.'

The same principle, Xenophon held, would apply in all areas of human work, simply because men and their needs are the same. In another of the books he wrote on his estates at Scillus, the *Oeconomicus*, the book of estate management, he put across this distinctive view with characteristic style and compelling vigour. It reflected his own experience running these estates under the shadow of Mount Olympus. Much of the book is concerned with technical farming matters and the organization of the estates. But Xenophon urged upon his readers the importance of leadership on large farm estates. 'Nobody can be a good farmer,' he said

> unless he makes his labourers both eager and obedient; and the captain who leads men against an enemy must contrive to secure the same results by rewarding those who act as brave men should act and punishing the disobedient. And it is no less necessary for a farmer to encourage his labourers often, than for a general to encourage his men. And slaves need the stimulus of good hopes no less, nay, even more than free men, to make them steadfast.

This general leadership ability, as relevant to agriculture as to politics or war, was often absent, he noted, in those who held positions of authority. Xenophon instanced the Greek warships of his day, which, it must be remembered, were rowed by free men and not by slaves.

> On a man-of-war, when the ship is on the high seas and the rowers must toil all day to reach port, some rowing-masters can say and do the right thing to sharpen the men's spirits and make them work with a will. Other boatswains are so unintelligent that it takes them more than twice the time to finish the same voyage. Here they land bathed in sweat, with

mutual congratulations, rowing-master and seamen. There they arrive with dry skin; they hate their master and he hates them.

Xenophon's mind ranged back to the generals he had known, who also differed widely from one another in this respect.

For some make their men unwilling to work and to take risks, disinclined and unwilling to obey, except under compulsion, and actually proud of defying their commander: yes, and they cause them to have no sense of dishonour when something disgraceful occurs. Contrast the genius, the brave and skilful leader: let him take over the command of these same troops, or of others if you like. What effect has he on them? They are ashamed to do a disgraceful act, think it better to obey, and take a pride in obedience, working cheerfully, every man and all together, when it is necessary to work. Just as a love of work may spring up in the mind of a private soldier here and there, so a whole army under the influence of a good leader is inspired by love of work and ambition to distinguish itself under the commander's eye. Let this be the feeling of the rank and file for their commander, then he is the best leader – it is not a matter of being best with bow and javelin, nor riding the best horse and being foremost in danger, nor being the perfect mounted warrior, but of being able to make his soldiers feel that they must follow him through fire and in any adventure.

'So, too, in private industries', Xenophon continued, 'the man in authority – bailiff or manager – who can make the workers keen, industrious and persevering – he is the man who gives a lift to the business and swells the profits.'

* * * * * * *

For Xenophon, this kind of leadership is quite simply 'the greatest thing in every operation that makes any demand on the labour of men'. If leaders are made in the sense that they can acquire the authority of knowledge, are they born as far as the capacity to inspire is concerned? It is tempting to conclude so. The ability to give people the intellectual and moral strength to venture or persevere in the presence of danger, fear or difficulty is not the common endowment of all men and women. Xenophon, however, did believe that it could be acquired through education, though not 'at sight or at a single hearing'. He was not specific about the content or methods of such an education for leadership, but Socratic discussion must have been one strand in it.

As Xenophon implied, some degree of leadership potential has to be there in the first place. Many people possess it without being aware of the fact. Given the need or opportunity to lead, some encouragement and perhaps a leadership course or programme, most people can develop this potential. Those with a greater amount of natural potential can correspondingly become greater leaders within their spheres, providing that they are willing to work hard at becoming leaders.

Learning about leadership happens when sparks of relevance jump in between experience or practice on the one hand, and principles or theory on the other hand. One without the other tends to be sterile. It is a common fallacy that leadership is learnt only through experience. Experience only teaches the teachable, and it is a school which charges large fees. Sometimes people graduate from it when they are too old to apply the lessons. Leadership is far better learnt by experience *and* reflection or thought, which, in turn, informs or guides future action. Other people, as examples or models, teachers or mentors, have an important part to play in this process. Socrates, for example, most probably acted as Xenophon's own mentor.

The belief that theories or principles, imbibed from books or courses, can by themselves teach a person to lead is equally a half-truth. All the academic study of leadership does is to teach one *about* leadership, not how to lead. It is certainly useful for people to clarify their concepts of leadership, either as a prelude or as an interlude in the practical work of leading others. But leadership is learnt primarily through doing it, and nothing can replace that necessary cycle of experiment, trial and error, success and failure, followed by reflection and reading. Following this path of self-development, a person may become so effective as a leader that it becomes, as it were, a second nature. Others may say 'He or she was born to it', but little will they know the work it took. It takes a long time to become a born leader!

* * * * * * *

4

Discovering the three-circles model

A picture is worth a thousand words.
CHINESE PROVERB

IN THE HEAT of the Egyptian summer, the Scots Guards moved south from their base camp near Port Said to guard and patrol a vast ammunition dump in the desert of the Canal Zone. My platoon was given the job of laying a dense and broad barbed wire barrier around a section of the ammunition dump. We had to drive out to where the fence ended with lorries loaded with the necessary materials, and then start work where our predecessors had left off. The dump was so large that we were out of sight of any buildings.

On the first day we laid about 20 metres of the complex barbed wire barrier. It was extremely hot and the guardsmen were far from happy. Next day I took off my shirt and worked with the men, knocking in stakes and fixing the coils of wire. By the day's end we had built about 80 metres of the entanglements. After supper that evening in my tent I worked out in my head several ways of doing the job faster, such as dumping stores in advance of the work. As a result, next day we laid even more wire. By the fourth day a remarkable change had come over the platoon: They were cheerful, keen, full of ideas, reluctant to stop work and eager to set a higher target for the fifth day. So it continued for the next two weeks.

For example, I noticed a big change in Guardsman McCluskey, a former Glaswegian gang member with a criminal record and a reputation as a real troublemaker back in camp. Here he emerged as a leader of a subgroup. He was enthusiastically still talking about ways of laying more wire if we could be allowed to obtain certain other types of equipment when the time came to hand over the job to the next platoon. 'You'll never lay 200 metres of wire in a day like *we* have just done', announced McCluskey to the newcomers. Nor did they!

Although I carried the scars of the barbed wire on my arms for several years, I looked back upon those days under the burning sun as happy ones. And in retrospect, too, I can see that in that experience lay the seeds of my discovery of the Three-Circles model.

At the time, to be honest, I attributed the success of the project almost entirely to the fact that I had 'led from the front', or led by example if you prefer, and shared the extreme heat and toil of the day with the soldiers. And doubtless at the time I was rather pleased with myself for having done so. But if so, I had fallen into an error. Over the course of time, my mind came up with a very different interpretation of why things went so well that day, thoughts that formed the groundwork of what became Action Centred Leadership.

For what I had observed for the first time – perhaps I should say experienced – is the dynamic interaction in work groups between progress on *task* and the cohesiveness of *team*. Also I had noticed the effects of that change on each *individual* involved. Guardsman McCluskey and myself are the examples of that phenomenon in this story.

And far from it being the case that my action of working alongside the men had galvanized them into working harder, what I had actually done as their leader was to perform some necessary functions, such as planning, controlling and coordinating, and encouraging. Working myself among the men had been, as it were, only the icing on the cake.

As you may have guessed, I am now calling on my own Three-Circles model and its associated functional approach to understand that desert experience, but in fact the development of the theory of it then lay about ten years away in my future.

Although some readers may be already familiar with this theory, let me outline it for you now.

Group personality and group needs

Work groups are more than the sum of their parts: They have a life and identity of their own. All such groups, providing they have been together for a certain amount of time, develop their own unique ethos. I call this phenomenon *group personality*, a phrase which I borrowed from the British prime minister Clement Attlee. Writing about the cabinet form of government, he says:

> It is interesting to note that quite soon a Cabinet begins to develop a group personality. The role of the Prime Minister is to cultivate this, if it is efficient and right-minded; to do his best to modify it, if it is not.

The other half of the theory stresses what groups share in common as compared with their uniqueness. They are analogous to individuals in this respect: Different as we are in terms of appearance and personality, we share in common our needs – at midnight all of us usually begin to feel tired, at breakfast time we shall be hungry and so on. According to my theory, there are three *areas of need* (Figure 4.1) present in working groups:

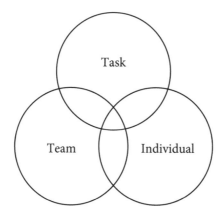

Figure 4.1 *The interaction of areas of need.*

- The need to achieve the *common task*

- The need to be held together or to *maintain itself as a cohesive unity*

- The *needs* which *each individual brings* with them into the group.

Task

One of the reasons why a group comes together is that there is a task which one person cannot do on their own. But does the group as a whole experience the need to complete the task within the natural time limits for it? A human being is not very aware of a need for food if they are already well fed, and so one would expect a group to be relatively oblivious of any sense of need if its task is being successfully performed. In this case the only sign of a need having been met is the satisfaction or elation which overtakes the group in its moments of triumph – a happiness which, as social beings, we often count among our deepest joys.

Before such fulfilment, however, many groups pass through a 'black night of despair', when it may appear that the group will be compelled to disperse without achieving what it set out to do. If the group's members are not committed to the common goal, this will be a comparatively painless event; if they are committed, the group will exhibit various degrees of anxiety and frustration. Scapegoats for the corporate failure may be chosen and punished; reorganizations might take place and new leaders emerge. Thus, adversity reveals the nature of group life more clearly than prosperity. In it we may see signs or symptoms of the need to move on effectively with whatever task the group has come together to do.

Team

The team maintenance need is not so easy to perceive as the task need: as with an iceberg, much of the life of any group lies below the surface. Again, it helps to think of groups which are threatened – from outside by forces aimed at their disintegration, or from within by disruptive people or ideas. We are then able to see how they give priority to maintaining themselves against these external or internal pressures, sometimes showing great ingenuity in the process.

Many of the written or unwritten rules of the group are designed to promote this unity and to maintain cohesiveness at all costs. Those who rock the boat, or infringe group standards and corporate balance, may expect reactions varying from friendly indulgence to downright anger. If you turn to page 24 above, you can see an example, drawn from Xenophon's account of the Persian expedition. Note that it is the group who discipline the recalcitrant Soteridas, not Xenophon the leader.

Instinctively, a common feeling exists that 'united we stand, divided we fall', that good relationships, desirable in themselves, are also an essential means towards the shared end. This need to create and promote group cohesiveness is what I refer to as the team maintenance need.

Individual

What is a team? The origin of the Old English word 'team' provides us with a clue: a set of draught animals, such as oxen, horses or dogs, harnessed together to pull a vehicle or implement. The word literally meant offspring or lineage, probably because it was found that animals pulled together better if they were related. So teamwork here is the combined action of a group of individuals, its drawing or pulling power. Notice that the importance of selection is already in the picture: only a *well-matched* group of animals produces teamwork that is effective and efficient.

In addition, individuals bring their own needs into the group – not just the physical needs for food and shelter (which nowadays are largely catered for by the payment of a salary) but also the psychological ones: recognition, a sense of doing something worthwhile, status and the deeper needs to give to and receive from other people in a working situation. These individual needs are perhaps more profound than what many people may realize.

Such needs spring from the depths of our common life as human beings. They may attract us to, or repel us from, any given group. Underlying them all is the fact that people need one another not just to survive but to achieve and develop personality. This growth occurs in a whole range of social activities – friendship, marriage and local community – but inevitably work groups are extremely important because so many people spend so much of their waking time operating within them.

The Three Circles interact

The Three-Circles model suggests quite simply that the task, team and individual needs are always interacting with each other. The circles overlap but they do not sit on top of one another. In other words, there is always some degree of tension between them.

Many of an individual's needs, such as the need to achieve and the social need for human companionship, are met in part by participating in working groups. But an individual can also run the risk of being exploited in the interests of the task and thus dominated by the group in ways that trespass upon one's personal freedom and integrity.

It is a fundamental feature of the Three-Circles model that each of the circles must always be seen in relation to the other two. As a leader you need to be constantly aware of what is happening in your group in terms of the three circles. You might imagine one circle as a balloon getting bigger (better) and another shrinking,

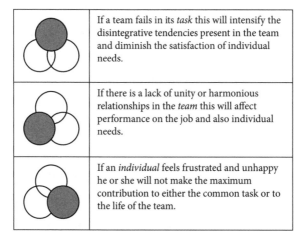

	If a team fails in its *task* this will intensify the disintegrative tendencies present in the team and diminish the satisfaction of individual needs.
	If there is a lack of unity or harmonious relationships in the *team* this will affect performance on the job and also individual needs.
	If an *individual* feels frustrated and unhappy he or she will not make the maximum contribution to either the common task or to the life of the team.

Figure 4.2 *The interaction of needs.*

or you may visualize the situation as if one circle is completely eclipsed or blacked out (Figure 4.2).

In perspective

Since the publication of my first book *Training for Leadership* in 1968, the Three-Circles model has been in the public domain for over fifty years. Remember that it is a theory about work groups, not about leadership as such – that belongs to the next chapter.

So far the theory has not been falsified. To do that, a critic would have to find a work group which lacked task, group (or team) and individuals, which is clearly impossible, or should be able to demonstrate that there are no positive or negative dynamic interactions between the three domains.

As far as I know, no one has made this second kind of objection to the Three-Circles model. In other words, the truth of it has not been questioned. Indeed, for many people it comes across as self-evident. 'The truth has such a face and such a mien', wrote John Dryden, 'as to be loved needs only to be seen.'

The originator of a theory is perhaps not the best person to evaluate it. But as far as I can tell, the various criticisms of my work have been directed at Action Centred Leadership rather than at the basic Three-Circles model that I have outlined in this chapter. Please feel free to correct me if I am wrong.

The value of the model is that it shifts attention away from the leader and on to the group. We see that a human work group is very different from a flock of sheep who merely play follow-the-leader. In the human context, can we then think of the leader's function as being simply to serve the group? Yes, to a large extent, but not entirely so.

5

The role of leader

*Human experience, which is constantly contradicting theory,
is the great test of truth.*

DR SAMUEL JOHNSON

THE THREE-CIRCLES MODEL forms the basis of my theory that there is a generic role of *leader* – a common set of responsibilities that can be found in all work groups.

First, however, it is important to understand the concept of *role*. By origin it is a theatrical metaphor: In its English form a *roll* was the paper that contained the actor's lines, his or her part in the play. In extended use, a *role* is a capacity in which someone acts in relation to others. In social contexts, it is often determined by the expectations of others. For example, we expect police officers or doctors to act professionally in characteristic ways. Therefore *role* implies appropriate conduct; it has a reference to a norm of behaviour built into it.

It is worth bearing in mind that the most enduring forms of social relations – those which are sufficiently repeated as to be classified under common names – however deeply personal they may be, are also role relations.

Notice, too, that role relations are always reciprocal. You cannot, so to speak, function as a doctor without a patient, or as a police officer without a citizen. To be a father, Socrates observes in Plato's *Symposium*, it is necessary to be *somebody's* father.

The common phrase 'role model' refers to a person who is regarded by others as an example in a particular role. The implication here, of course, is that the person so described is a *good example*.

Rivers of academic ink have flowed in trying to determine the difference between a leader and a manager. But this debate has proved to be entirely fruitless because it rests upon a basic category mistake, a term introduced by the distinguished Oxford University philosopher Gilbert Ryle in his classic text *Concept of Mind* (1949).

Ryle gives some colourful examples to illustrate the meaning of a category mistake. For example, he talks about a cricket match, where all the players and their roles are being described by an English host to a foreign guest. 'I do not see whose role it is to exercise *esprit de corps*,' she says. Her mistake is to think that exercising team spirit is a specific function in the game, rather than being a manner or spirit in which specific functions are performed.

Another example of a category mistake is to confuse a generic term, one relating to a class or group, with the specific. Pears, apples and peaches are examples of specifics in the class of fruit. You can eat all of them but it would be a category mistake to order 'fruit' for that purpose.

Following this metaphor, 'leader' is the equivalent to 'fruit', and terms like 'manager', 'company commander', 'director', 'conductor', 'chairman', 'chief executive', 'prime minister', 'president' and 'king' are all specifics.

Therefore you'll never meet anyone in the street who is *just* a leader, just as you'll never meet anybody who is *just* a father or mother, brother or sister. What you may meet, for example, is a nurse who is a leader, an engineer who is a leader or a musician who is a leader.

Before outlining the generic role of *leader*, there is one more important distinction that needs to be made: between the position or office of a leader – the role itself – and the ability to fulfil it.

The frequent confusion between these two factors goes back to the 1820s, when the word 'leadership' was first coined and subsequently found its way into the English vocabulary.

As I have already mentioned, the word breaks down into three elements: LEAD-ER-SHIP. Each of these elements taken separately predates the 1820s by a thousand years. Shakespeare, for example, found the term 'soldiership' already available in the English language.

The last suffix, –*ship*, is ambiguous, for it can indicate position, status or rank – as in lordship or dealership on the one hand, or, on the other hand, skill, ability or art, as in craftsmanship or horsemanship. So when we talk about the leadership of the trade unions or about business leaders, we are referring to those in charge: those who occupy the highest positions or offices of responsibility. There is no implication either way as to their ability to lead others.

The Three-Circles model is like the double helix: just as the latter opened the door for scientists to map human genes, so it enabled me to identify the key functions that constitute – without exhausting – the generic role of *leader*. And that in turn opened another door: the possibility of using the knowledge for training, more specifically, training for leadership.

The logic for applying the theory in this practical way rested on two grounds. The first ground is that, being simple, it is very time efficient, for *generic* roles can be taught effectively within two or three days. It is then up to the student – using that word in its broadest sense – to apply it to the *specific* role they already occupy or will in the future. And, as in all fields of human enterprise, time is money.

The second ground is that it works. In order to support that contention, I shall provide some evidence, after I have done some initial outlining.

One last word in this introduction about the name 'Action Centred Leadership'. At Sandhurst and in the other armed services during the 1960s, this approach was known as Functional Leadership. In 1970, when the Industrial Society adopted it for training foremen, supervisors and managers, John Garnett, the Industrial Society's director, gave it the new name of Action Centred Leadership (which in turn, in those acronym-fashionable days, led to 'ACL'). As more than a million managers participated in the Industrial Society's ACL courses in the UK and overseas, the name gradually eclipsed the older 'Functional Leadership', even (eventually) in the armed services.

Over the past fifty years, however, Action Centred Leadership has ceased to be a brand name and has become far more of a generic term. It is a development that I welcomed, because my general theory of leadership (as outlined in the next chapter) embraces more than just a functional approach.

* * * * * * *

Does an orchestra need a conductor? Does a choir need a choirmaster? Could a ship function without a captain? Theoretically, all are possible. In practice, however, it is a fact that work groups tend to have leaders. Even if there is no appointed or elected leader with a title, informal leaders will emerge in order to address the three overlapping areas of need. Their responsibilities mirror the Three-Circle model, but they are expressed in functional or active terms (see Figure 5.1).

Figure 5.1 *The generic role of leader.*

It is no accident that *Achieving the task* is the top circle, for the leader bears – relative to the others – the greatest share of responsibility for success. As Field Marshal Lord Slim said,

> Defeat is bitter. Bitter to the common soldier, but trebly bitter to his general. The soldier may comfort himself with the thought that, whatever the result, he has done his duty faithfully and steadfastly, but the commander has failed in his duty if he has not won victory – for that is his duty. He has no other comparable to it. That's what requires him to give his country victory – or at the very least, stave off the worst consequences of defeat.

What is less obvious is that – not unlike an iceberg – beneath the surface there are two other areas of leadership responsibility: for the teamwork, morale and *esprit de corps* of the whole, and for each individual in terms of the content of the work.

One of the strongest reasons for teaching leaders – or aspiring leaders – at all levels about the generic role of the *leader* is that, without that knowledge, and left to their own devices, those in positions of leadership tend to hone in on the task exclusively, at the expense of people.

It is, of course, not the case that the leader should give an equal attention to all the circles all the time – that would demonstrate a complete misunderstanding of the model. Situations dictate priorities. But a real leader never completely forgets team and individual needs. After a time of necessary immersion in the task – perhaps in an unforeseen crisis – they will re-engage with the team and the individuals.

In order for the three overlapping areas of leadership responsibility to be met, certain functions need to be performed. A *function* is what you *do*, as opposed to a *quality*, which is what you *are* or what you *know*. We are now firmly into action centred territory.

Functions are a form of what philosophers call 'middle actions': for they are concepts that occupy the middle ground between what is (too) abstract or general and what is (too) concrete or specific. In other words, they are bridges between the Three Circles and the day-to-day activities of the leader. And on a bridge, the traffic can always move in both directions.

It is precisely because the Three Circles overlap that I prefer to work with one set of functions rather than three. This is because any one functional act can affect all three areas – one more directly, the other two more indirectly. For example, there is nothing like a bad plan – or sometimes, a lack of any planning – to divide a work group into factions or to frustrate individual members.

The list of functions below is purely indicative; I have never felt it incumbent upon me to provide a definitive list and then to require rigid adherence to it. There are, however, some functions that will always appear on any list. What do you think they are (see Figure 5.2)?

Defining the task	What are the purpose, aims and objectives? Why is this work worthwhile?
Planning	A plan answers the question of *how* you are going to get from where you are now to where you want to be. There is nothing like a bad plan to break up a group or to leave individuals feeling demotivated.
Briefing	The ability to communicate: to ensure that people have understood both the task and the plan.
Controlling	Making sure that all resources and energies are properly harnessed.
Supporting	Setting and maintaining organizational and team values and standards.
Informing	Bringing information to the group and from the group: that is, the *linking* function of leadership.
Reviewing	Establishing and applying the success criteria appropriate to the field.

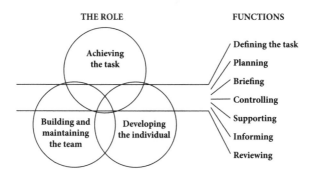

THE ROLE   FUNCTIONS

Achieving the task

Building and maintaining the team

Developing the individual

Defining the task
Planning
Briefing
Controlling
Supporting
Informing
Reviewing

Figure 5.2 *Leadership functions.*

Notice that our direction of travel is from the simple (the Three Circles in Figure 5.1) to the more complex (the set of functions in Figure 5.2).

There is an analogy of this process of moving from the simple to the complex in the analysis of light. Light refracts into three primary colours: red, green and blue. With the colours formed by the overlaps of these primary colours, we arrive at the spectrum of colours we associate with the rainbow (conventionally red, orange, yellow, green, blue, indigo and violet) (see Figure 5.3).

To follow the analogy one step further, the complex moving pictures on the channels of our television screens are made up of an ever-changing kaleidoscope of dots and these seven colours, that is, if you like, a picture of your busy day. If, however, like an artist, you stand back from the picture, you can see the ever-changing kaleidoscopic patterns of *task*, *team* and *individual*.

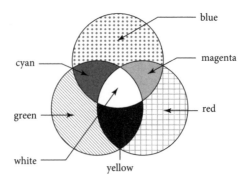

Figure 5.3 *The colour spectrum.*

The test of time

If you consider the theory behind Action Centred Leadership –
the Three-Circles model and the generic role of leader – it
is extremely difficult to know how the truth of it could be
established. Perhaps the only clue lies in a principle advanced by
Einstein in *Out of My Later Years* (1950):

> Ethical axioms are found and tested not very differently
> from the axioms of science. Truth is what stands the test
> of experience.

Or, as the Roman proverb put it more succinctly, *truth is the
daughter of time.*

Einstein once attended a lecture by the philosopher Karl
Popper, who himself had a lasting influence on both the

philosophy of science and, more generally, epistemology, the science that deals with the origin and method of knowledge. At the heart of his contribution is the simple principle: that scientific hypotheses and theories can never be finally confirmed as true. All that can be said of them is that they have survived all attempts to falsify them.

By that criteria, I can report that the theory of Action Centred Leadership, which has been in print and in the public domain now for over fifty years, still awaits falsification. The one serious attempt to subject it to a searching critical examination by a group of academics left it entirely unscathed: in other words, so far so good.

Action Centred Leadership proper is a combination of the theory outlined above and group-centred training methods. If we take just one example – the British Army – it has been taught and has been in continual use since 1964. No other leadership theory known to me has been subjected to – and survived – that length of time in service. According to the Ministry of Defence publication *Army Leadership Doctrine* (2016), Action Centred Leadership is now officially the Army Leadership Model:

The Army Leadership Model. Extensive consultation has determined that the most relevant leadership model that concisely summarises the role of the Army leader is Adair's theory of Action Centred Leadership™. It is a theory which has endured the tests of time, is applicable at all levels of leadership, and accessible to all ranks. With some minor adaptation to acknowledge the importance of understanding the context, Action Centred Leadership™ has been adopted as the Army Leadership Model.[1]

Although there remains an element of truth in the proverb *Leaders are made not born* – people do differ in their natural potential for leadership – what Action Centred Leadership has proved beyond reasonable doubt is that it is both possible and feasible to train for leadership. A sure foundation for future learning can be laid. This finding has given solid substance to Field Marshal Lord Slim's confident words:

> There is nobody who cannot vastly improve his powers of leadership by a little thought and practice.

---

[1] J Gosling, P Case and M Witzel (2007). *John Adair: Fundamentals of Leadership*, Basingstoke: Palgrave Macmillan.

6

A general framework

Dust as we are, the immortal spirit grows
Like harmony in music; there is a dark
Inscrutable workmanship that reconciles
Discordant elements, makes them cling together
In one society
WORDSWORTH

THE FUNDAMENTAL QUESTION about leadership is, *Why is it that one person rather than another is perceived to be – or accepted as – a leader by others?*

In the history of the world there have been three main approaches to answering that question. They are not exclusive, however, and so I have represented them here as interlocking pieces of a jigsaw puzzle, which together make a whole (Figure 6.1).

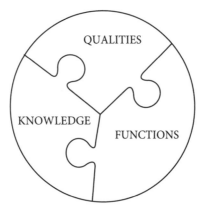

Figure 6.1 *The three approaches.*

The Qualities Approach

'It is a fact that some men possess an inbred superiority which gives them a dominating influence over their contemporaries, and marks them out unmistakably for leadership.' So an eminent churchman, Dr Hensley Henson, Lord Bishop of Durham, told his audience at the University of St Andrews. 'This phenomenon is as certain as it is mysterious,' he continued.

It is apparent in every association of human beings, in every variety of circumstances and on ever plane of culture. In a school among boys, in a college among students, in a factory, shipyard, or a mine among the workmen, as certainly as in the Church and in the Nation, there are those who, with an assured and unquestioned title, take the leading place, and shape the general conduct.

These words were spoken in 1934 – the year, incidentally, that Adolf Hitler became head of state in Germany, taking the title of *Führer*. The bishop believed, as most people thought then, that leadership was a form of 'inbred superiority' – in other words, you are either born with it or not. The born leader would emerge naturally as the leader because he (note the assumption that leaders are men) has innate qualities that give him such an 'assured and unquestioned title'. Such a leader could presumably lead in any circumstance or situation.

The first list of these 'innate qualities' of leadership in the English language appears in Shakespeare's *Macbeth*. At that time, the word 'leadership' did not exist, though Shakespeare does call some generals 'men of great leading'. The prime function of a king in those days was to lead his army from in front into battle as epitomized by his role model of kingship, Henry V. So we can take it that his 'king-becoming graces' are essentially leadership qualities. They are twelve in number:

> *The king-becoming graces,*
> *As justice, verity [truthfulness], temperance, stableness,*
> *Bounty [generosity], perseverance, mercy, lowliness [humility],*
> *Devotion, patience, courage, fortitude.*

Not until 1912 do we find another list comparable to it, this time in prose and pitched at an audience of aspiring young people. An anonymous booklist, priced at sixpence and entitled *How to be a Leader of Others*, deduces ten qualities from the study of great leaders (a category which, incidentally, in 1912 included the German emperor: 'A strong-willed and inspiring leader, able to secure the affection and obedience of his subjects'). The qualities offered as a framework for self-cultivation included confidence, ambition, self-reliance, energy, personality, courage, dignity, magnetism, coolness and self-discipline.

Although the reader is exhorted to work hard – really hard – over a long period of time, no advice is given on how this self-help should be managed or undertaken. Nor are there any examples of those who have successfully completed the course. In fact all programmes to build one's character by a direct assault on a selected set of personal traits is self-defeating.

There is another problem, arising from what has been called the law of indirection. Once you specify a set of the qualities of leadership, there arises in your mind or the minds of others another quality not on the list which also claims attention as being important. Why leave out, for example, resilience, tact, courtesy or a sense of humour? So lists of leadership qualities have tended to get longer and longer as time goes by.

Rather like our use of the word 'values' in conversation, the term 'leadership qualities' works reasonably well. We sort of know what the other person means by them. Difficulty only arises when we ask the question: 'What *are* these qualities?' In other words, how are we to know which of the various lists is the correct one?

Even a quick comparison shows that the two lists outlined above have only one quality in common – courage. That doesn't help us very much, as all soldiers – and arguably all humans at certain times in their lives – need courage. So why call it a leadership quality?

Empirical studies by psychologists served to confirm the confusion. For example, a study by Professor Charles Bird of the University of Minnesota in 1940 looked at twenty experimental investigations into leadership and found that only 5 per cent of the traits described appeared in three or more of the lists.

The difficulty, then, is that the lists vary so considerably, even allowing for the fact that the compilers are often using rough synonyms for the same trait. In fact, there is a bewildering number of trait names from which the student of leadership could make up their own portfolio. There are some 17,000 words in the English language that can be used for describing personality or character.

A questionnaire survey of seventy-five top executives, carried out by the American business journal *Fortune*, listed fifteen executive qualities: judgement, initiative, integrity, foresight, energy, drive, human relations skill, decisiveness, dependability, emotional stability, fairness, ambition, dedication, objectivity and cooperation. Nearly a third of the seventy-five said that they thought all these qualities were indispensable. The replies showed that these personal qualities have no generally accepted meaning. For instance, the definitions of 'dependability' included 147 different concepts.

The difficulty is lessened if we limit the broad term 'quality' – in the sense of a *qualification* – to the narrower concept of a *trait* of personality or character. That means consciously setting aside attributes of the mind, such as intelligence, creativity, curiosity and judgement. Also to be left out of the picture is any form of acquired knowledge or skill.

In my thinking about these residual personal traits, I have introduced distinctions between 'personality' and 'character', two terms that are often lumped together or otherwise confused. Personality denotes the overall emotional impression that a person makes upon you, especially on a first meeting. Character, by contrast, is not immediately apparent. It only reveals itself over time, as you get to know another person – or yourself for that matter – better. Character denotes a person's moral being, as evidenced in such qualities as honesty, integrity and moral courage. You may have noticed that we never apply the terms 'good' or 'bad' (in their moral sense) to anybody's personality. Instead, we use qualifiers such as 'pleasant' or 'unpleasant', 'attractive' or 'unattractive', 'optimistic' or 'pessimistic'.

There is a further distinction that needs to be made between, on the one hand, trying to compile a list of the traits of personality and character that leaders actually possess and, on the other, the qualities that they *ought* to have.

The first of these exercises is doomed to failure. Having written two biographies myself and read countless others, I know full well just how difficult it is to capture personality and character in words. For we are, in Shakespeare's words, 'mixed yard'. In reality, any given is a complex mixture of strengths and weaknesses, and great leaders tend to have great strengths and great weaknesses.

Once the generic role of *leader* has been discovered and mapped, the second exercise – identifying the qualities of personality and character which 'become' that role, adding value and substance to it and making it personal – becomes a lot easier.

But how exactly does one do it? This is where art has to supplement science in our understanding of leadership, for there is no scientific way of doing it. A clue lies in this observation by Proust:

> The writer, in order to attain generality and, so far as literature can, reality, needs to have seen many churches in order to paint one church, and for the betrayal of a single sentiment, he requires many individuals.

In other words, it is necessary to draw on a wide study and observation of leaders, past and present, and across many fields of human endeavour. Even then any list of leader-becoming qualities will always be tentative and incomplete: I call it *indicative*. As a result, this means you are entirely free to add to or subtract from it as you please. Here are the qualities that have remained constant in my own mind:

Enthusiasm (Chapter 7)

Integrity (Chapter 8)

Tough and demanding but fair (Chapter 9)

Warmth and humanity (Chapter 10)

Humility (Chapter 11)

The Situational Approach

Why is it that one person in a group is perceived to be and accepted as the leader? According to the Situational Approach, the answer is simple: It all depends on the situation. As some research in 1947 concluded, 'There are wide variations in the characteristics of individuals who become leaders in similar situations and even great divergence in different situations. The only common factor appeared to be that leaders in a particular field *need and tend to possess superior general or technical competence* or knowledge in that *area*' (italics author's).

The origins of the Situational Approach go back deep in history to Socrates in Athens in the fifth century BCE. Socrates wrote no books. Our main sources of information about him are Plato's *Dialogues*, Xenophon's *Memorabilia* and the satirical picture painted by Aristophanes in *The Clouds*. It is uncertain how far Plato and Xenophon attributed their own opinions to their common master. When it comes to the theme of leadership, it is especially difficult to determine how much goes back to Socrates. Xenophon himself was both a leader and a thinker about leadership. Did he put his own views into the mouth of Socrates? He certainly wrote in the form of Socratic dialogues, with Socrates as one of the speakers. Or, when as a young man he heard Socrates cross-examining various would-be leaders, did he take notes? These questions cannot be answered with any degree of confidence, but at least we know of one core idea in Xenophon, which does go back to Socrates – that leadership is tied to situations and depends largely upon the leader having the appropriate knowledge; we know this because Plato also takes up that theme.

THE PARABLE OF THE SHIP'S CAPTAIN

The sailors are quarrelling over the control of the helm. ... They do not understand that the genuine navigator can only make himself fit to command a ship by studying the seasons of the year, sky, stars and winds, and all that belongs to his craft; and they have no idea that along with the science of navigation, it is possible for him to gain, by instruction or practice, the skill to keep control of the helm whether some of them like it or not.

Plato, *The Republic*

The same theme emerges in a dialogue that Xenophon records between Socrates and a newly elected young cavalry commander. (Was it Xenophon himself?) Socrates asked him first why he had sought that office. The young man agreed that it could not have been because he wanted to be first in the cavalry charge, for the mounted archers usually rode ahead of the commander into battle, nor could it have been simply in order to get himself known to everyone – even madmen achieve that. The aspiring commander then accepted Socrates' suggestion that his aim must be to leave the Athenian cavalry in better condition than when he found it. Xenophon, both a renowned authority on horsemanship and the author of a textbook on commanding cavalry, had no difficulty in explaining what needs to be done to achieve that end. The young commander, for example, must improve the quality of the cavalry mounts; he must school new recruits – both horses and men – in equestrian skills and then teach the troopers their cavalry tactics.

'And have you considered how to make the men obey you?' continued Socrates. 'Because without that, horses and men, however good and gallant, are of no use.'

'True, but what is the best way of encouraging them to obey, Socrates?' asked the young man.

'Well, I suppose you know that under all conditions human beings are most willing to obey those whom they believe to be the best. Thus in sickness they most readily obey the doctor, on board ship the pilot, on a farm the farmer, whom they think to be most skilled in his business.'

'Yes, certainly,' said his student.

'Then it is likely that in horsemanship too, one who clearly knows best what ought to be done will most easily gain the obedience of the others.'

Xenophon captures here a very distinct theme in Socrates' teaching on leadership. In harmony with the rest of the doctrine of Socrates (for, despite his pose of ignorance, Socrates had ideas of his own), it emphasizes the importance of *knowledge* in leadership. People will obey willingly only those whom they perceive to be better qualified or more knowledgeable than they are in a particular situation.

Xenophon elsewhere gives us a vivid example of the Situational Approach in action. It relates to the emergence of Clearchus of Sparta as the commander-in-chief of the Ten Thousand after their disastrous defeat on the field of Cunaxa. Although he had ingrained soldiership qualities you would expect in a Spartan, neither in personality nor in character – his persona – could the veteran general be described as an attractive man. Yet he became the man for the hour.

Clearchus took it upon himself to act as spokesman for his fellow generals to the Persian emissaries, but gave no indication to anyone what he was going to say. After sunset he summoned a meeting of the officers, briefly reviewed the options and then told them what they must do. They must head northwards that very night on the first stage of a long march to safety on the shores of the Black Sea, which lay some 800 miles away. As Xenophon records in *The Persian Expedition* everyone sensed that only Clearchus could lead them out of mortal danger:

> On receiving their instructions the generals and captains went away and carried them out; and from then on Clearchus was in command, and they were his subordinates. This was not the result of an election, but because they realised that he was the one man who had the right sort of mind for a commander, while the rest of them were inexperienced.

Spartans such as Clearchus were renowned for using few words. One English word for that kind of terse speech is 'laconic', which derives from the Greek name for Sparta. The best kind of authority is quiet authority. For, as Leonardo da Vinci once said, 'He who knows truly has no need to shout.'

Nor, incidentally, should you draw attention to yourself by any reference to your own leadership. Remember the Chinese proverb: *Tigers do not proclaim their tigritude.* If others refer to you spontaneously as a leader, or comment on your leadership, it is an accolade – not one to bestow upon yourself. You can say that you write verse or that you attempt to write poetry, but only others can say if you are a poet.

The Functional Approach

Whereas the Qualities Approach draws attention to what you *are* and the Situational Approach to what you *know*, the focus of the Functional Approach is upon what you need to *do*.

As I have already presented the Functional Approach comprehensively in the foregoing chapters, I shall not repeat myself here.

* * * * * * *

Pulling the threads together

By combining all three approaches, a first and very provisional definition of a leader begins to take shape:

A leader is the sort of person with the appropriate *qualities* and *knowledge* – which is more than technical or professional – who is able to provide the necessary *functions* to enable a team to achieve its task and to hold it together as a working unity. And this is done not by the leader alone but by eliciting the contributions and willing cooperation of all involved.

Of course, it is one thing to weave together the three constituent theories of leadership into one general theory, as I have done. But it is quite another exercise for a person to integrate them into their daily practice of leadership *without thinking about it*. Yet it can and does happen, for our unconscious mind does much of this holistic work for us, a process well captured in the quotation which stands at the head of this chapter.

You do, however, need to be patient. As Xenophon observed long ago, the work of becoming a leader is not done in a day.

In a lecture I once heard him give, Admiral Sir Richard Clayton used the analogy of 'the ship that found itself' in a short story by that name written by Rudyard Kipling. 'This tells of a brand new well-found ship setting out on her maiden voyage. She meets her first storm, and all her separate bits – the beams and stringers and plates and rivets – start chattering and talking to each other. To begin with there is argument about who is the most important and who is doing the most work. But slowly the bits bed in and start to work together; and as they do so, the individual voices disappear, to be replaced by the single strong voice of the ship – the ship that has found itself.'

From time to time we do need to remind ourselves where the ship is heading.

Dag Hammerskjöld, then secretary general of the United Nations, kept a private notebook to help himself stay on course as a leader and thus to fulfil the expectations of the world for his great office. One evening, in the solitude of his apartment in New York, he wrote for his own benefit these words:

Remember that your position does not give you the right to command. It only lays upon you the duty of so living your life that others may receive your orders without being humiliated.

7

Enthusiasm

The very life-blood of our enterprise
WILLIAM SHAKESPEARE

WHY IS ENTHUSIASM so important in a leader? A clue lies in the original Greek word *enthuousiasmos*, which literally means to be possessed by a god, or – as we would say – to be inspired. Enthusiasm is contagious. Think about it. If you are not inspired yourself, how can you expect to inspire others?

To enthuse or inspire others, then, is to arouse in them an enthusiasm for the common purpose that matches your own. Admiral Lord Nelson (1758–1805) had a natural gift for this kind of leadership, a fact which became immediately apparent to those whom he met – officers and seamen alike.

Prince William, for example, who later became King William IV, remembered his first meeting with Nelson, then a twenty-three-year-old frigate captain, in this vivid picture:

I was then a Midshipman on board the *Barfleur*, lying in the Narrows off Staten Island, and had the watch on deck, when Captain Nelson of the *Albemarle*, came in his barge alongside, who appeared to be the merest boy of a captain I ever beheld; and his dress was worthy of attention. He had on a full laced uniform; his lank unpowdered hair was tied in a stiff Hessian tail, of an extraordinary length; the old fashioned flaps on his waistcoat added the general quaintness of his figure, and produced an appearance which particularly attracted my notice; for I had never seen anything like it before, nor could I imagine who he was, nor what he came about. My doubts were, however, removed when Lord Hood introduced me to him. There was something irresistibly pleasing in his address and conversation; and an enthusiasm when speaking on professional subjects, that showed he was no common being.

That enthusiasm for cause, country and profession remained with Nelson until his last moments. But it was not a shallow enthusiasm, a mere trick of personality. It came with Nelson's other natural abilities as a leader and an immense capacity for hard work in day-to-day naval administration. As Admiral Collingwood once said of his lifelong friend, 'Nelson possessed the zeal of an enthusiast, directed by talents which Nature had very bountifully bestowed on him, and everything seemed, as if by enchantment, to prosper under his direction. But it was the effect of system, and nice combination [a coordinated and effective sequence of actions], not of chance.'

After one successful action when Nelson was still a young captain, his commander-in-chief Admiral Lord St Vincent wrote him a letter which contains this compliment:

> I never saw a man in our profession who possessed the magic art of infusing the same spirit into others which inspire their own actions. ... All agree there is but one Nelson.

* * * * * * *

Good leaders *are* enthusiasts. They tend, therefore, to generate in others the same wholehearted commitment to the task in hand as they exhibit in their own attitude and actions. And, as Xenophon first pointed out, such leaders make a difference in *any* form of human enterprise, not just war on land, sea or air. This kind of leadership, he says, is quite simply 'the greatest thing in every operation that makes any demand on the labour of men'.

Although Xenophon did believe that leadership could be acquired through education, though not 'at sight or at a single hearing', he was not specific about the content or methods of such an education for leadership, but Socratic discussion of the kind that he had personally experienced with the master must have been one strand in it. Yet when it comes to enthusiasm, Xenophon falls back – as it were – on the root of the Greek word: *en + theos*, possessed by a god or divine spirit:

> Above all, he must be a genius, a person possessed by a tutelary spirit. For I reckon this gift is not altogether human, but divine – this power to win willing obedience: it is manifestly a gift of the gods to the true votaries of wisdom. Despotic rule over unwilling subjects they give, I fancy, to those they judge worthy to live the life of Tantalus, of whom it is said that in hell he spends eternity, dreading a second death.

* * * * * * *

In distant China, Xenophon's near contemporary the Master Kung, known to us by his Latin name Confucius, had opened the world's first academy for educating the leaders of tomorrow. He, too, showed a great awareness of the importance of securing a harmonious wholeheartedness among the people. His message can be summed up in Emerson's words: *Nothing great is achieved without enthusiasm.*

Many of the teachings of Confucius became encapsulated in Chinese proverbs. Here is one of them:

> *When people are of one mind and heart,*
> *they can move Mount Tai.*

Tai is a mountain in what is now the Shandong Province, the largest one known to Confucius.

The clearest statement from Confucius on the need for leaders to inspire enthusiasm in their people – and therefore, by implication, to be enthusiastic themselves – comes in another conversation with his neighbour and friend, the chief minister of his own state of Lu.

> Chi K'ang Tzu asked, 'How can one inculcate in the common people the virtue of reverence, of doing their best and of enthusiasm?'
> The Master said, 'Rule over them with dignity and they will be reverent; treat them with kindness and they will do their best; raise the good and instruct those who are backward and they will be imbued with enthusiasm.'

It is the length of the journey that induces weariness and a flagging of spirits in many people. They lose their vision and their enthusiasm along the way. The best leaders, however, never give up; they remain whole-souled in the work at hand, however demanding. If they do feel the pace and the going is rough, they don't show it.

> Tzu-lu asked about government. The Master said, 'Encourage the people to work hard by setting an example of yourself.'
> Tzu-lu asked for more. The Master said, 'Do not allow your efforts to slacken.'

Tzu-chang asked about government. The Master said, 'Over daily routine do not show weariness, and when there is action to be taken, give of your best.'

Notice how Confucius applies enthusiasm – sustained enthusiasm – even to the domain of daily routine, or, to widen the term, administration. For him, there is no divide between the work of a leader and manager or administrator. If a manager of routine work shows enthusiasm and energy to the day's end, he or she is more than a manager – they are leaders.

* * * * * * *

'When a man is eager and willing, the gods join in.' So said the earliest Greek dramatist Aeschylus, a contemporary of Confucius. Enthusiasm is simply the quality in a leader that enables him or her to infuse others with the same spirit of eagerness and willingness that animates themselves.

8

Integrity

Trust being lost, all the social intercourse
of men is brought to naught.
LIVY, ROMAN HISTORIAN

THE PRIMARY MEANING of integrity is wholeness or soundness. Integrity implies a unity – an interdependence of parts and completeness or perfection of the whole. But integrity also means adherence to a set of moral, artistic or other values, especially truth, that are – so to speak – outside oneself. And so integrity is closely related to an undeviating honesty in what you say or do. Therefore it is entirely incompatible with any form of insincerity. Consider the personal ideal that Mahatma Gandhi set before himself: 'What you think, what you say and what you do are in harmony.' It is a good star for all leaders to follow.

A person of integrity, then, is honest to such a degree that they are incapable of being false to a trust, responsibility or pledge – or to their own standards of conduct. For integrity is the opposite of a condition where a person can be moved by opportunist or self-seeking impulses, which threaten to break up his or her unity as a whole being.

It is a wholeness which stems from being true to truth. We know what it means when people say of a scholar or artist that he or she has integrity. They do not deceive themselves or other people. They are not manipulators. As Oliver Cromwell once said in a letter to a friend, 'Subtlety may deceive you, integrity never will.'

The critical importance of adhering to truth in the context of leadership – and indeed in all personal relations – is that it creates and maintains trust. Mutual trust between the leader and the led is absolutely vital: Lose that and you have lost everything. Moreover, it is very hard to re-establish it. As the Roman poet Catullus says, 'Trust, like the soul, once gone, is gone for ever.'

Just why is it that people who have integrity in this sense create trust in others, I shall leave you to reflect upon at your leisure. Certainly, we all know that a person who deliberately misleads us by telling lies sooner or later forfeits our trust. It is a leadership principle which those political leaders of nations who lie to their people have been – and are – slow to learn, or have chosen to ignore. They do so in the naive belief that this time they will be able to get away with it. But they are often found out in the long run, often greatly to their discomfort: for the truth has a way of surfacing into the light of day, however deeply it has been buried in the ground, at dead of night.

* * * * * * *

Our world today is plagued by those who practise bribery and corruption or countenance it in others: two sides of the same coin. Corruption, namely, being influenced by using bribery or indulging in any kind of fraudulent activity, is rampant worldwide for one simple reason: Many people occupying roles of leadership are not leaders in the true sense of the word – they are imposters. The discovered instances of their corruption, or other signs of moral depravity, are merely symptoms of their lack of integrity, the backbone of true leadership.

Here the elections of representative democracy are a limited tool for weeding out candidates for high office who are deficient when it comes to personal and professional integrity. The reason lies in the difference between personality and character. Personality is up front – we can see, feel and assess it. Character is hidden; no one can judge it at first sight, only over the course of time, in the trials and tribulations of office. Plutarch, the Greek writer of the second century CE, described the unfortunate

Roman politician Gaius Antonius, elected to the highest office in Rome, as 'a man with no aptitude for leadership in any direction, either good or bad'. And it was said of the Roman emperor Galba that everyone thought he would make a great emperor until he actually occupied the office.

Confucius observed the same phenomenon in his own time and place, which suggests that it is a universal problem:

> What about men who are in public life in the present day?
> The Master said, 'Oh, they are of such limited capacity that they hardly count.'

Does this mismatch between holders of the office of leadership and leadership ability matter? Clearly Confucius thought that it did. Otherwise why would he go to such lengths to sow the seeds of a new kind of leadership in China, providing advice for the sages of tomorrow?

Does it matter today? Of course it does. More so, in fact, because the consequences of the lack of leadership in public life – in politics and business life, not least in that form of economic management we call banking – reverberate throughout the world. In our complex and interdependent world, vulnerable to disruption, few things are more important than the quality and credibility of leaders.

* * * * * * *

Confucius is insistent upon the importance of trustworthiness in a leader, and he recognized that in order to inspire others' trust, a leader must have integrity.

> The Master said, 'Duke Wen of Chin was crafty and lacked integrity. Duke Huan of Ch'i, on the other hand, had integrity and was not crafty.'

We can assume that Duke Wen was not acceptable to Confucius – how could he be? For integrity certainly implies, among other things, being trustworthy or reliable in word. It is not an exaggeration to say that Confucius regards integrity as the linchpin of moral character; indeed he uses that very metaphor:

> The Master said, 'I do not see how a man can be acceptable who is untrustworthy in word. When a pin is missing in the yoke-bar of a large cart or in the collar-bar of a small cart, how can the cart be expected to go?'

'Integrity without knowledge is weak and useless, and knowledge without integrity is dangerous and dreadful', Dr Samuel Johnson once said. Clearly integrity on its own is never going to be enough: It is the foundation but not the actual house of leadership.

A willingness to stand up to a powerful head of state when he or she begins to lead in the wrong direction is the test of a minister's integrity, but it applies beyond the realm of government to all working contexts. All team members, associates or colleagues should be fearless in speaking the truth to their leaders if the occasion calls for it:

> Tzu-lu asked about the way to serve a lord. The Master said, 'Make sure that you are not being dishonest with him when you stand up to him.'

For Confucius the foundation of any government is the trust of the people. He had the wisdom to see that this principle applied in all States, whatever their form of government. Ultimately, he perceived, any government depends upon the trust if not the consent of the people.

And, as Confucius tirelessly taught, rulers ignore this principle at their peril. However well a government provides for the protection of its people or for its sustenance, if it neglects the mutual trust between itself and its subjects, the very foundation of a civilized society is threatened.

> Tzu-kung asked about government. The Master said, 'Give them enough food, give them enough arms, and the common people will have trust in you.'
>
> Tzu-kung said, 'If one had to give up one of these three, which should one give up first?'
>
> 'Give up arms.'
>
> Tzu-kung said, 'If one had to give up one of the remaining two, which should one give up first?'

'Give up food. Death has always been with us since the beginning of time, but when there is no trust, the common people will have nothing to stand on.'

In leadership, example is everything. As the Moorish proverb says, *When the shepherd is corrupt, so is his flock.*

Chi K'ang Tzu succeeded his father as the chief minister of Confucius' home in the native state of Lu in 492 BCE, holding office for more than twenty-five years. On several occasions he sought advice from a neighbour already renowned for his practical wisdom.

The prevalence of thieves was a source of trouble to Chi K'ang Tzu who asked the advice of Confucius. Confucius answered, 'If you yourself were not a man of desires, no one would steal even if stealing carried a reward.'

The phrase 'a man of desires' is rather obscure. In this context, it probably means outright greed, covetousness and corruption. They all amount to what is essentially theft, for a corrupt ruler, minister or official is in effect stealing money from their own people. They are as guilty as a common thief, even though the act takes place in secret and all too often escapes the kind of scrutiny that leads to justice.

Confucius, as always, stresses to those who came to him for guidance on how to become good leaders and leaders for good, the power of good example. The higher you are, he implies, the longer your shadow – the influence of the example you provide. If people see those occupying positions of leadership taking their own illegal or immoral shortcuts to wealth, for example, by seeking out bribes or by acting corruptly in other ways, will they not be tempted to follow suit? Of course they will, especially if they see their betters getting away with it. Such is the power of bad example.

Given, however, good example on the part of their leaders, few people will resort to theft or – by extension – to corrupt practices. And this will be the case even if – Confucius adds, doubtless with a smile – they were offered a considerable reward for doing so.

Is it true? Does it work? Of course it does. The prophet Muhammad and the first four caliphs of Islam, for example, led simple lives and were scrupulous in all financial matters, and corruption was unknown in the Muslim states of their day. The first president of Botswana and his three successors set their faces against corruption, and as a result Botswana became the least corrupt nation in Africa.

*　*　*　*　*　*　*

Political leaders with such integrity shine like stars in their generation, however dark the sky may be. Of Joseph Addison (1672–1719), for example, who held political office, his friend and fellow poet Alexander Pope could write:

Statesman, yet friend to truth; of soul sincere,
In action faithful, and in honour clear;
Who broke no promise, serv'd no private end,
Who gain'd no title, and who lost no friend.

Such a statesman was George Washington (1732–99), first president of the United States and an example of uprightness to all his successors – some of whom have dropped the torch. In a letter to James Madison, Washington writes, 'It is an old adage that honesty is the best policy. This applies to public as well as private life, to states as well as to individuals.'

The presence of strong ambition in a person – I mean, ambition in the pejorative sense of an inordinate striving after rank and wealth – will usually test their integrity. For the promise of shortcuts to the top at the expense of one's moral values is sometimes just too tempting. Yet those who sacrifice their integrity upon the altar of ambition may well live to regret it bitterly. As a Chinese proverb expresses it, *he who sacrifices his integrity to achieve his ambition burns a picture to obtain the ashes.*

* * * * * * *

You must be the change that you
wish to see in the world.
MAHATMA GANDHI

9

Tough and demanding but fair

To my God,
A Heart of Flame;
To My Fellow Human Beings,
A Heart of Love;
To Myself,
A Heart of Steel

ST AUGUSTINE

ON SABBATICAL LEAVE during my time at Sandhurst I spent a year as the first director of studies at St George's House in Windsor Castle. One of my tasks was to design and deliver a first-ever course designed to equip selected clergymen to be future leaders of the Church of England. Mainly for the purposes of winning support for the project, I met a selection of the diocesan bishops then in office. One of them, the bishop of Manchester, gave me a list of what he considered to be the six top priorities for the Church. On the list I noticed 'Care for the Dying'.

'How do you do that?' I asked the bishop.

'I do not know,' he replied.

That evening in St George's House I noticed after a supper a tall young woman standing alone in the drawing room where coffee was served. In conversation she told me that, having worked for some time as a nurse, she had recently qualified as a doctor. Her special interest was care for the dying – as it was expressed in those days – and with quiet enthusiasm she shared with me her vision for a great expansion of hospices in the UK and the world at large. Her name, I discovered, was Cicely Saunders.

Thanks largely to Cicely's leadership over the coming years, the hospice movement came into being and has won widespread public support. In the course of time the National Portrait Gallery in London commissioned a portrait of Dame Cicely Saunders and she attended the unveiling ceremony. One of her friends stood beside her, looking at the portrait. 'Cicely,' she eventually said, 'I hope you don't mind me saying so but you do look rather severe.'

'Yes,' replied Cicely Saunders, 'yes, I suppose I do – *love and steel*.'

* * * * * * *

All real leaders have both those elements in them: love and steel. By 'steel' I mean toughness, which means firm, strong, not easily broken or in this context resilient. You may recall that in Xenophon's judgement the Greek general Proxenus, for example, lacked toughness (p. 38).

The toughness in a leader should not be arbitrary: It should be a reflection of the toughness or demandingness of the task. Remember that the Three Circles overlap. If a leader demands the impossible and thereby secures the best in the Task circle, then there will be transformational effects in the Team and Individual circles. Nowhere is this principle better illustrated than in the domain of orchestral music.

* * * * * * *

While I was at St Paul's School, which is a day school, Sir Thomas Beecham used the empty great hall on Saturday mornings to rehearse the Royal Philharmonic orchestra. With his permission I watched these rehearsals with my attention on Beecham as a leader.

What fascinated me was how Beecham achieved results with so few words. Speaking in retrospect much later on, one of the orchestra's members – the celebrated clarinettist Jack Bryman – put his finger on it: 'For Beecham, conducting was a silent, choreographic art. When he turned his eye on you, you knew exactly how it had to be. Most of his magic was in his eye – it wasn't in his beat.'

Another great conductor, Otto Klemperer, also expected the best from his players. He was not given to show his feelings, but after one rehearsal he was pleased enough with the result to turn as he walked off the stage and say with a smile 'Good.' After a few moments of silent surprise, the delighted orchestra rose as one to its feet and burst into applause. Klemperer, who had resumed his walk, turned again and said, 'Not *that* good.'

What Klemperer, I think, is doing quite spontaneously is to stop the orchestra from becoming pleased with itself: for to be great, an orchestra needs great humility. In music one occasionally touches the stars but there is no dwelling place there.

Sir Neville Marriner, who once played an instrument in his early years as a musician in the London Symphony Orchestra, remembers the impact on them of Leopold Stokowski, a British-born American conductor of Polish descent:

> In about three days he managed to transmit to us the notion that we were a great orchestra. It gave us enormous confidence and we suddenly realised, in one concert at the Festival Hall, that we could achieve, had just achieved, a great performance – that we could achieve it just as easily as any other orchestra in the world. I think it was a great turning point for the orchestra suddenly to be given this confidence in one performance.

From that moment the LSO never looked back – it was extraordinary. What did he do? He put more responsibility on the players than they had before. He more or less said to them, 'This is your orchestra and if you want it to be good, then you must perform. I will do my best to make it happen but the responsibility is yours.' He just had this remarkable ability to focus the emotion of an entire orchestra. His personality was immensely strong.

This element of demandingness in a conductor can produce great performances. As Sir Georg Solti says,

> In my enthusiasm and intensity I will very often push people to the limits of their capabilities – and that must entail a certain degree of risk. The great thing is that the risk pays off when that person suddenly finds something in themselves they didn't know was there.
>
> I believe, particularly with great musicians that I'm able to collaborate with, that the sky should be the limit. And therefore as I am prepared to take the risks and shoot for the limit, then why shouldn't they follow?

The best conductors are actually not the egoistical ones, who present themselves and not their orchestras as the star of the show. Like Lau Tzu's excellent leader – 'When his work is done, the people will all say "We did this ourselves"' – the greatest conductors are self-effacing. And in this respect they are a model for the modern leaders at all levels. It is well expressed by the eminent American-Estonian conductor Paavo Järvi:

> Success as a conductor has nothing to do with movement. It has everything to do with persona, the personality and a person's ability to communicate with the musicians and convey your ideas. The strength of the performance comes in conveying your involvement in the process, rather than being a god who wields the whip with the capacity to open and close the door. You must be someone who embraces and helps the orchestra. The most effective leadership, to me, is the leadership that doesn't look like leadership. The moment somebody walks in looking and sounding like a 'leader', that's quite suspicious to me. You must be part of the process – so convinced by what you are doing that everyone else has no choice but to follow you. It's intuition and personality. You have to encourage people to open up, seduce them, not scare them, to follow you. That's a great leader!

Toughness and demandingness, however benign their purposes, need to be balanced by justice and fairness. Justice derives from the Latin *jus*; 'fair' is Old English by origin. Although in modern English they have slightly different connotations, essentially they refer to the same thing. The Roman lawyer Justinian expressed it in a nutshell: *Justice is the constant and unceasing will to give everyone their right or due.* A distinguished lord chief justice of England, Lord Denning, described justice as a spiritual thing with no satisfactory or precise definition, though as a working definition he proposed that '*it was what right-thinking men and women believe to be fair*'.

Equivalence, the equal value of giving and taking, seems to be a guiding norm in human relations, which isn't to say that it's always the case. As you may have observed, few human relations have perfect symmetry in this respect; they may have it for a time, but time and change have a way of altering the balance.

There is certainly a case for saying that our instinct for equivalent reciprocity is a matter of nature and nurture. I find it fascinating that in the first six months of a human baby's life its mother hands objects to the baby and the baby takes them. Gradually the baby is encouraged to hand them back. By the time the baby is about twelve months old these exchanges involving giving and receiving have become more or less equal. The exchange of smiles probably follows the same pattern. Gorilla mothers and their babies do not exhibit this particular pattern of behaviour with their young. But then personality is not a gorilla attribute, or at least only in vestige.

There are two broad types of contracts: spoken or written contracts, and unspoken or unwritten contracts. The former are *explicit* agreements, sometimes exactly spelt out in all their details, so that there is no room for ambiguity or reason for difficulty in interpretation. Work for lawyers here! An *implicit* 'contract' by contrast is left largely unexpressed. As a general principle, the more impersonal the relation, the more we tend to make the contract explicit. The more personal the role relation – as in those we experience within families and among friends or neighbours – the more we rely upon unspoken mutual understanding and trust: for roles are composed of mutual expectations, which include fairness. All children expect equal slices of the birthday cake.

It is an error to think of justice and fairness – that hidden impersonal element in our role relations with each other – as being antithetical, inferior or second-best to personal relation. The proper connection between them is that the former is a necessary condition for the latter. It is the base line in the music, and music is perfect harmony. William Temple, the archbishop of Canterbury during the Second World War, captures this principle for us:

> Justice is the first expression of love. It is not something contrary to love, which love mitigates and softens. It is the first expression of it that must be satisfied, before the other and higher expressions can rightly find their places.

Or, as Thomas Aquinas says, 'Grace does not destroy nature, but perfects it.'

You should remember, however, that justice and fairness – like all the other 'king-becoming graces' – are what philosophers call *regulative ideals*. They serve to inspire or give direction to our behaviour and to prevent our minds from falling into error. But in practice we shall not get it right every time – be it fairness or love.

Take courage to persevere, however, from Tolstoy's insight. Yes, we are human beings and not gods. Yes, we sometimes miss the mark where justice or fairness is concerned. Yet nonetheless there is a real difference between a just person and an unjust one, between a loving person and an unloving one. As Tolstoy says,

> Not a single person can be completely just in all his deeds, but a just person can be completely different from an unjust one with his efforts, in the same way as a truthful man is different from a liar, with his efforts to speak only truth.

10

Warmth and humanity

That best portion of a good man's life,
His little, nameless unremembered, acts
Of kindness and of love
WORDSWORTH

LIVES OF LEADERS are not without record of such small acts of kindness. For the ambitious and scheming Lady Macbeth in Shakespeare's play – as for all Machiavellians – the kindness she sensed in her husband she sees as a weakness. 'Yet I do fear your nature,' she tells him. 'It is too full of the milk of human kindness to catch the nearest way.'

Kindness is the quality of being interested in the welfare of others, sympathetically concerned for their well-being and compassionate for them when they fall into need, want or any other affliction. In other words, it is the humanness or the humanity appropriate to man as a rational, social and sensitive being. And, like a mother's milk, the 'milk of human kindness' is warm when it is served: touch, warmth, food.

In the context of the Three-Circles model, the quality of kindness most often appears in relation to the Individual Needs circle. In normal circumstances an individual's needs are met – in one way or another – by participation in Task and Team. But individual persons are ends as well as means. That is the reason, incidentally, why the Individual circle appears as the same size as the Task and Team in the Three-Circles model.

* * * * * * *

A captain who served with Admirals Nelson and Collingwood describes them as being 'as hard as their rudder posts, men who regarded a hail of round shot as if it had been a shower of snowflakes'. But, he added, 'They are as tender-hearted as schoolgirls.' And Collingwood in turn said of Nelson, 'In private life he was kind.'

One day, for example, Nelson had himself rowed over from his flagship the *Victory* to a frigate at anchor nearby where two poor fellows, suspected of shamming madness in order to secure an early discharge, were lying secured in iron chains after both had attempted to commit suicide. Nelson sat down beside them and listened to their stories. He then offered to pay £50 out of his own pocket (the equivalent today of £4,000) to send the younger seaman, whose mental illness he thought might be curable, to a hospital for treatment. Both men he discharged from the service on compassionate grounds.

On another occasion Nelson went out of his way to help the wayward son of one of his closest comrades, a recently discovered letter reveals.

Three weeks before the Battle of Trafalgar, on 29 September 1805, Captain Charles Tyler told Nelson over dinner on the HMS *Victory* that his son, Lieutenant Charles Tyler, had run off with a dancer from Malta. Nelson wrote the next day to the captain, reassuring him 'we shall get hold of [your son] before any great length of time'.

Lieutenant Tyler was tracked down to a debtors' prison in Naples, and Nelson wrote to a contact, Captain Frank Sotheran, asking for his release. Nelson paid the lieutenant's debt with his own money.

As both these stories illustrate, Nelson exemplified yet another one of Shakespeare's 'king-becoming graces' – *bounty* or gracious liberality. Such a warm-hearted generosity often walks hand in hand with compassion.

In public – on the quarterdeck – leaders such as Nelson and Collingwood wear the mask of command. Both officers and seamen observed a social distance, a disciplined adherence to roles that made friendly intercourse possible but forbade the ease of address we call familiarity. It was a lesson of leadership which newly appointed officers learnt by example – good or bad.

As a young lieutenant in the Royal Navy in the days of Nelson, William Dillon experienced this kind of familiarity. On one occasion, for example, he saw two or three seamen enter the captain's cabin on his frigate 'with as much freedom as if in their own homes and spoke to their Captain in the most familiar tones. He seemed to encourage all that, as he styled them Tom, Jack and Bill. My plan of proceeding', continues Dillon, 'was diametrically opposed to this. There is a certain deportment which, regulated by *firmness and moderation*, never fails to produce its object. Upon that principle I avoided abusive language, but never failed to rebuke the negligent.' He finished his career as Admiral Sir William Dillon.

Collingwood, like Dillon, avoided abusive language and he insisted that his officers and warrant officers did likewise. He insisted that they address seamen by name or as 'sailor', refrained from swearing at them or striking them with a rope's end or cane. On his ships mutual respect was the order of the day.

In my service in the Scots Guards, incidentally, I found much the same. Discipline of the nature that Dillon describes actually creates freedom – freedom for a certain friendliness off duty which carries no danger of familiarity. There is a good example from the Brigade of Guards in the Crimean War (1853–6).

On that campaign Colonel Hood of the Grenadier Guards reprimanded his young adjutant Captain George Higginson on more than one occasion. Once, for example, when Higginson had provided food for the men and left them sitting down to eat,

Hood told him off because he had not waited to see if they had had enough to eat.

A few days after that particular incident the Grenadiers were manning the trenches before Sevastopol; a Russian cannon ball struck Colonel Hood in the chest, instantly killing him. That evening Higginson took up his pen to write a letter of condolence to Hood's widow:

> We have lost the man whose firmness and calm leadership were so conspicuous at the battle of Alma. … Though of reserved nature, he yielded it freely at times, to a love of friendly intercourse. I had lived on terms of the greatest intimacy with him, and although he treated me in all matters of duty with a sternness approaching severity, his kindly bearing and language while we were enjoying our simple meals together confirmed my early belief that in him I had found a true friend.

That same note of warm friendliness pervades a letter of Captain Alexander Schomberg (1720–1804), commanding officer of the thirty-two-gun HMS *Diana*, written while he was on station in the West Indies. It is addressed to a seaman called William Page, who lost a hand in an accident when firing a cannon. While recovering in England, Page had written to his captain requesting a warrant from him so that he could become a cook – the post traditionally occupied by seamen who had lost an arm or a leg while at sea. Schomberg replies:

My lad, I have received your letter of the 28th of January and take this first opportunity in answering it. Get your petition written out and specify your accident in it and send the enclosed letter to Mr Cleveland Sec at the Admiralty and I make no doubt that your business will be done. I am going to sea the first wind that offers and I shall be glad to hear that you are provided for. I am, my lad, your friend and well-wisher.

* * * * * * *

One unintended consequence of such 'little, nameless, unremembered acts of kindness and of love' is that word somehow or other gets around about the inner character of the leader in question. And, as we are reciprocal beings, it evokes a like response. That British fleet that sailed into action at Trafalgar, for example, shared in common a love for Admiral Lord Nelson.

As Plutarch said in the first century CE, 'evidence of trust begets trust, and love is reciprocated by love.' Sixteen centuries later, the English divine Richard Baxter echoes his words:

I saw that he that will be loved must love; and he that rather chooses to be more feared than loved, must expect to be hated, or loved but diminutively. And he that will have children, must be a father; and he that will be a tyrant must be content with slaves.

11

Humility

Knowledge is proud that he has learned so much;
Wisdom is humble that he knows no more
WILLIAM COWPER

TO BE HUMBLE means to be markedly lacking in all signs of pride, arrogance, self-assertiveness or vanity. Whereas modesty is a trait of personality – soon revealed in the way a person talks about himself or his achievements – humility is a quality of character. It is only by getting to know a person well can you sense the presence of humility in them.

It actually is not easy to do so, because humbleness is not evidenced by such outward signs as unsolicited self-deprecation – the act of disparaging or belittling oneself. There are celebrities who, in Shakespeare's words, 'sound all the base notes of humility' but privately are as proud as Satan.

C. S. Lewis, as lucid as ever, in *Mere Christianity* (1952) points to the hiddenness of this quality:

Do not imagine that if you meet a really humble man he will be what most people call 'humble' nowadays: he will not be a sort of greasy, smarmy person, who is always telling you that, of course, he is nobody. Probably all you will think about him is that he seemed a cheerful, intelligent chap who takes a real interest in what *you* said to *him*. If you do dislike him it will be because you feel a little envious of anyone who seems to enjoy life so easily. He will not be thinking about humility: he will not be thinking about himself at all.

Dag Hammarskjöld is perhaps the leader in modern times who has reflected most deeply on the meaning of humility. In Hammarskjöld's private journal, humility is a central theme. Later published posthumously in Swedish with the title of *Väg Märken* ('Way Marks') – such as the stone cairns that guide the fell walker on snowbound or mist-shrouded paths – and in English as *Markings*, the journal contains, for example, this observation on humility.

29.7.59

Humility is just as much the opposite of self-abasement as it is of self-exaltation. To be humble *is not to make comparisons*. Secure in its reality, the self is neither better nor worse, bigger nor smaller, than anything else in the universe. It *is* – is nothing, yet at the same time one with everything. It is in this sense that humility is absolute self-effacement.

The great Japanese potter Hamada referred to humility as 'losing one's tail' – the tail being an excessive egoism. Incidentally, there is a fine distinction in the English language between *egoism* and *egotism*. *Egoism* emphasizes a concentration on oneself, one's interests and one's needs; it commonly implies self-interest, especially as opposed to altruism or interest in others, as the inner spring of one's acts or as the measure by which all things we judge.

Egotism stresses the tendency to attract attention to and centre interest on oneself, one's thoughts or one's achievements. It is a trait difficult to disguise as it is manifest in the practice of continually talking about oneself, usually with an excessive use of 'I' and 'me'.

A SHORT COURSE ON LEADERSHIP

The six most important words: 'I admit I made a mistake.'
The five most important words: 'I am proud of you.'
The four most important words: 'What is your opinion?'
The three most important words: 'If you please.'
The two most important words: 'Thank you.'
The one most important word: 'We.'
And the least important word: 'I.'

* * * * * * *

President Dwight D. Eisenhower emphasized the value of humility in leadership: for, he said, 'a sense of humility is a quality I have observed in every leader whom I have deeply admired.'

> My own conviction is that every leader should have enough humility to accept, publicly, the responsibility for the mistakes of the subordinates he has himself selected and, likewise, to give them credit, publicly, for their triumphs. I am aware that some popular theories of leadership hold that the top man must always keep his 'image' bright and shining. I believe, however, that in the long run fairness and honesty, and a generous attitude towards subordinates and associates, pay off.

The leadership that Eisenhower displayed as the supreme commander in Europe in the closing years of the Second World War reflected these values. In the words of Cambridge University's Public Orator when an honorary degree was conferred upon Eisenhower: 'He showed himself such an example of kindly wisdom, such a combination of serious purpose, humanity, and courtesy, that the others soon had no thought in their minds save to labour with one common will for the success of all.'

* * * * * * *

'Any leader worth his salt', Eisenhower adds, 'must of course possess a certain amount of ego, a justifiable pride in his own accomplishments. But if he is a truly great leader, the cause must predominate over self.' An old and respected commander of mine used to say, 'Always take your job seriously, never yourself.'

We find that very same principle – job first, self second – expressed by one of the great political orators of the nineteenth century, William Ewart Gladstone (1809–98), prime minister of England:

> We are to respect our responsibilities, not ourselves.
> We are to respect the duties of which we are capable, not our capabilities simply considered.
> There is to be no complacent self-contemplation, ruminating on self.
> When the self is viewed, it must always be in the most intimate connexion with its purpose.

Gladstone sounds the same note as Eisenhower: the priority of one's role as leader in a great office as being the overriding context for any considerations of self or about self.

That advice given to Eisenhower by his old and respected friend underlines the importance of a leader, especially at the most senior levels: retaining their sense of humour, for humour keeps things in proportion; it is the antidote to any form of self-importance.

Lady Violet Bonham Carter, a friend who overcame her negative critical reaction to Churchill's personality and grew to admire and like Churchill, once said to him: 'Winston, you must remember that you are just a worm, like the rest of us.' Churchill thought for a moment and then replied with a characteristic chuckle: 'Yes, I am a worm – but I do believe that I am a *glow-worm*!'

If you feel that humility is beyond your reach, make sure that you hang on to a sense of humour!

Sense shines with double lustre when it is set in humility. An able yet humble man is a jewel worth a kingdom.

WILLIAM PENN

12

The strategic leader

Dux erat ille ducum (He was leader of leaders)
OVID (43 BC– AD 17/18), HEROIDES

A STRATEGIC LEADER is essentially the leader of an organization. An *effective* strategic leader is one who delivers the goods in terms of what an organization naturally expects from its leadership in times of change.

There is an underlying unity in strategic leadership, whatever field you are in and however structured or unstructured your work in it may be. Walter Bagehot, a nineteenth-century banker, economist and journalist famous for his insights into economics and political questions, understood this well:

> The summits of the various kinds of business are, like the tops of mountains, much more alike than the parts below – the bare principles are much the same; it is only the rich variegated details of the lower strata that so contrast with one another.

But it needs travelling to know that the summits are the same. Those who live on one mountain believe that their mountain is wholly unlike all others.

A Chinese proverb expresses this truth more succinctly:

There are many paths to the top of the mountain
But the view is always the same.

Therefore you can draw lessons and insights from many sources in order to grow as a strategic leader. In order to do so, however, you do need *a wide span of relevance*. By that I mean that we naturally look for examples or case studies in our own field, such as business or education, and think that these ones alone are relevant to our situation. But you should be able to see relevance to your situation in the examples of, say, an orchestral conductor or a Greek general. It is the same principle, incidentally, that lies behind creative thinking: The sparks of meaning jump between two or more apparently unconnected things to produce new ideas. It is also fun to think like this.

Military origins of strategic leadership

Originally, strategy (*strategia* in Greek) meant strategic leadership – the art of being a commander-in-chief.

'Strategy' is in fact made up of two ancient Greek words. The first part comes from *stratos*, which means an army spread out as in camp, and thus a large body of people. The second part, *-egy*, comes from the Greek verb 'to lead'. There is a rough breathing mark in the Greek, giving an *h* sound, which explains the spelling of the English word 'hegemony' – meaning the leadership of one nation over others – which is derived from it.

The issue emerges clearly in a conversation that Socrates – according to Xenophon – once had with a soldier called Nicomachides.

'Why', retorted Nicomachides, 'merchants also are capable of making money, but that doesn't make them fit to command an army!'

'But', replied Socrates, 'Antisthenes also is eager for victory, and that is a good point in a general. Whenever he has been choir master, you know, his choir has always won.'

'No doubt', conceded Nicomachides, 'but there is no analogy between the handling of a choir and of an army.'

'But you see,' said Socrates, 'though Antisthenes knows nothing about music or choir training, he showed himself capable of finding the best experts in these activities. And therefore if he finds and prefers the best men in warfare as in choir training, it is likely that he will be victorious in that too; and probably he will be more ready to spend money on winning a battle with the whole state than on winning a choral competition with his tribe.'

'Do you mean to say, Socrates, that the man who succeeds with a chorus will also succeed with an army?'

'I mean that, whatever a man directs, if he knows what he wants and can get it he will be a good director, whether he directs a chorus, an estate, a city or an army.'

'Really, Socrates,' cried Nicomachides, 'I should never have thought to hear you say that a good businessman would make a good general!'

By his familiar method of patient cross-examination, Socrates then proceeded to secure agreement from Nicomachides that successful businessmen and generals perform much the same functions. Then Socrates proceeded to identify six of these functions or skills:

- Selecting the right person for the job;

- Punishing the bad and rewarding the good;

- Winning the goodwill of those under them;

- Attracting allies and helpers;

- Keeping what they have gained;

- Being strenuous and industrious in their own work.

'All these are common to both', Nicomachides eventually agreed, but added, 'but fighting is not.'

'But surely both are bound to find enemies?' said Socrates.

'Oh yes, they are.'

'Then is it not important for both to get the better of them?'

'Undoubtedly, but you don't say how business capacity will help when it comes to fighting.'

'That is just where it will be most helpful,' Socrates concluded. 'For the good businessman, through his knowledge that nothing profits or pays like a victory in the field, and nothing is so utterly unprofitable and entails such heavy loss as a defeat, will be eager to seek and avoid what leads to defeat, will be prompt to engage the enemy if he sees he is strong enough to win, and, above all, will avoid an engagement when he is not ready.'

Levels of leadership

An army of a thousand is easy to find, but how difficult to find a general.
CHINESE PROVERB

Leadership is discernible on three broad levels: team, operational and strategic. These constitute a natural hierarchy in all working organizations, although in practice the levels tend to overlap and may be subdivided in a variety of ways.

Fortunately the same generic role of leader – the Three-Circles model and key general functions – applies at all levels. What changes with level, of course, is the *complexity* factor – complexity, incidentally, in all three circles, as the environment is constantly changing. Leading an *organization* is therefore both similar to and very different from a small *work group*. Thus, each level carries with it a more complex set of functional responsibilities.

Strategic	The leader of a whole organization, with a number of operational leaders under one's personal direction.
Operational	The leader of one of the main parts of the organization, with more than one team leader under their control. It is already a case of being a leader of leaders.
Team	The leader of a team of up to twenty people with clearly specified tasks to achieve.

A simple recipe for organizational success is to have excellent – well, at least effective – leaders occupying these roles and working together in harmony as a team. That is simple enough to say: I am not implying that it is easy either to achieve or to maintain that state of affairs under the pressures of life today. But what is your alternative?

Incidentally, you should always aspire to be a team and operational leader in spirit if not in office when you become a strategic leader. For instance, you should naturally create teamwork in the top group, which will include the senior operational leaders, so that it spreads out and infuses the whole organization.

Moreover, strategic leadership includes overall accountability for the operation of the organization – in the business context that means delivering the right goods or services, whatever they may be, at the right time and at the right price: for, as the proverb says, *an acre of performance is worth a world of promise.*

The functions of strategic leadership

The core role at any level refracts into broad functions derived from the Three-Circles model that we explored in Chapters 4 and 5. With the three meta-functions – Achieving the Task, Building the Team and Developing the Individual – in mind, then, there seems to me to be seven generic *functions* of strategic leadership. In my books *Effective Strategic Leadership* (2002) and *Strategic Leadership* (2010) I describe and illustrate these functions in full but here is a brief outline of them:

- Providing direction

    Knowing where the organization needs to be going. The three signposts here are *purpose*, why or for what general end does the organization exist; *vision*, what ought it to look like in, say, three to five years' time; and *values*, the moral compass. You steer by values as if they are stars, but you never reach them – they are not destinations.

- Getting strategy and policy right

  Strategy is the route to the longer-term destinations; it is concerned with what is important as opposed to urgent in the context of that longer-term state towards which the organization should be aiming. Strategy here encompasses both strategic thinking and strategic planning. Policies are general decisions that help others lower down to save time in decision-making.

- Making it happen

  The operational or executive function of strategic leadership, which includes getting out of the office to inspect what is happening, monitoring progress and reviewing performance against agreed targets in the strategic plan. Remember, results speak louder than words.

- Organizing and reorganizing as necessary

  Ensuring that the relation of the whole to the parts of the organization is optimum for the task in hand.

- Releasing the corporate spirit

  Encouraging and enthusing people at every level and, where possible, releasing the latent spiritual energy in people. The symptom of success here is high morale at every level and in every branch.

- Relating the organization to other organizations and to society as a whole

  Finding allies or partners among other organizations, sometimes by mergers and takeovers, and creating a spirit of cooperative teamwork with them; promoting excellent relations between the organization and the local, regional, national and/or international communities.

- Choosing today's and developing tomorrow's leaders

  Selecting the best operational and team leaders is a critically important function. The strategic leader should also 'own' a strategic plan (evolved with the head of human resources and the top leadership team) for improving leadership capability throughout the organization. Have a passion for developing leaders!

As I mentioned, the role and responsibilities are fundamentally the same at all levels of leadership and in all fields of work. What changes at the different levels is the degree of complexity that the leader faces. That complexity not only affects the nature of the task – the transition from what the military call tactics to the level of strategy. People seem more complex the older and more 'political' they get, and that new political dimension – both in its positive and negative senses – can probe and test any strategic leader's powers of leadership.

There is an end-product of real leadership: the high-performance team. Whether you are leading a team at the front-line level, or a significant part an organization, or the organization as a whole, the evidence of your effectiveness lies in the quality of the team that you build, maintain and lead by example. In that context, here are the key success criteria:

Remember that your key responsibility is to build a high-performance leadership team – strategic, operational and team leaders – in your organization.

The eight hallmarks of a high-performance team

Clear, realistic and challenging objectives

The team is focused on what has to be done – broken down into stretching but feasible goals, both team and individual. Everyone knows what is expected of them.

Shared sense of purpose

This doesn't mean that the team can recite the mission statement in unison! Purpose here is energy plus direction – what engineers call a vector. It should animate and invigorate the whole team. All share a sense of ownership and responsibility for team success.

Best use of resources

A high-performance team means that resources are allocated for strategic reasons for the good of the whole. They are not seen as the private property of any part of the organization. Resources include people and their time, not just money and material.

Progress review

The willingness to monitor their own progress and to generate improvements characterizes excellent teams. These improvements encompass process – *how* we work together – as well as tasks – *what* we do together.

Building on experience

A blame culture mars any team. Errors will be made, but the greatest error of all is to do nothing so as to avoid making any! A wise team learns from failure, realizing that success teaches us nothing and continual success may breed arrogance.

Mutual trust and support

A good team trusts its members to pursue their part in the common task. Appreciation is expressed and recognition given. People play to each other's strengths and cover each other's weaknesses. The level of mutual support is high. The atmosphere is one of openness and trust.

Communication

People listen to one another and build on one another's contributions. They communicate openly, freely and with skill (clear, concise, simple and tactful). Issues, problems and weaknesses are not sidestepped. Differences of opinion are respected. Team members know when to be very supportive and sensitive, and when to challenge and be intellectually tough.

Riding out the storms

In times of turbulent change it is never going to be all plain sailing. When unavoidable storms and crises arise, an excellent team rises to the challenge and demonstrates its sterling worth. It has resilience.

* * * * * * *

Heading such a high-performance team in any field feels like a privilege and it imbibes in all but the most egoistic among us a sense of humility.

Group Captain Leonard Cheshire (1917–92), for example, who was awarded the Victoria Cross – Britain's highest award for gallantry – for his leadership of bomber squadrons in the Second World War and who then went on to found the Cheshire Foundation Homes for the severely disabled, captured this spirit in a sentence:

> Leaders there have to be, and these may appear to rise above their fellow men, but in their hearts they know only too well that what has been attributed to them is in fact the achievement of the team to which they belong.

In working with such a high-performance team – however small or large it may be – the true leader sees themselves as no more than equal partners in the common enterprise, as what the ancient Romans called a *primus inter pares*: *first among equals.*

Leaders, like orchestral conductors, are there to enable all the voices or instruments to be heard to their best effect in harmony. Their role as leaders within their specific fields is to identify, develop and use all the talents of their people in a creative symphony of service to the common good.

A leader is best,

When people are hardly aware of his existence,

Not so good when people praise his government,

Less good when people stand in fear,

Worst, when people are contemptuous.

Fail to honour people, and they will fail to honour you.

But a good leader, who speaks little,

When his task is accomplished, his work done,

The people say, 'We did it ourselves!'

LAO TZU, SEVENTH CENTURY BCE

13

Practical wisdom

*Reason and calm judgment, the qualities
especially belonging to a leader.*
TACITUS

IN ORDER TO guide a group, organization or nation in the right direction, a leader needs the ability to think clearly and to decide when the time comes. It could be called the intellectual dimension of leadership.

Practical reason, intuition and imagination are all included under that heading. But it is not only a matter of the leader having some or all of these attributes. He or she has to be able to guide a decision-making body, such as a board of directors, whose members may have different mental abilities as well as different personalities and characters.

Decision-making meetings need to be chaired in an effective, business-like way. The atmosphere of the group matters, too, when it comes to thinking together for results. A good leader will remain 'cool, calm and collected', and by their example encourage others to do so. If things go wrong, he or she accepts full personal accountability.

The core activity is undoubtedly *thinking*. The Canadian entrepreneur Roy Thomson, who built up a vast publishing empire and owned *The Times*, insisted upon its importance. In *After I Was Sixty* (1975), his autobiography, he wrote:

> Thinking is work. In the early stages of a man's career it is very hard work. When a difficult decision or problem arises, how easy it is, after looking at it superficially, to give up thinking about it. It is easy to put it from one's mind. It is easy to decide that it is insoluble, or that something will turn up to help us. Sloppy and inconclusive thinking becomes a habit. The more one does it the more one is unfitted to think a problem through to a proper conclusion.
>
> If I have any advice to pass on, as a successful man, it is this: if one wants to be successful, one must think; one must think until it hurts. One must worry a problem in one's mind until it seems there cannot be another aspect of it that hasn't been considered. Believe me, that is hard work and, from my close observation, I can say that there are few people indeed who are prepared to perform this arduous and tiring work.

Roy Thomson clearly had a degree of natural *intelligence*. And to that he added both knowledge and experience in the decision-taking in his particular field. 'To be good at anything', he writes, 'requires a lot of practice, and to be really good at taking decisions you have to have plenty of practice at taking decisions. The more one is exposed to the necessity of making decisions, the better one's decision making becomes.'

If things go well there are seldom lessons learnt; failure, mistakes and mishaps tend to be far more instructive. They force us to review our thought processes: 'Where did I go wrong?' And this sort of experience – 'knowledge of good by knowing ill' – is fed into the cumulative formation of your judgment. The only real failure is not to learn from your failure. If you do, then, *all is grist to the mill* of your ever-turning mind, as Thomson discovers: 'I have had to take some important decisions, and, particularly in the early days, I often got these wrong. But I found later that the early mistakes and, for that matter, the early correct decisions, stood me in good stead. Most of the problems that I was confronted with in London were in one way or another related to those earlier ones.'

No leader has written more clearly than Roy Thomson about the role that the unconscious mind plays in the continuous process of judgment. He compares his mind in this respect to the workings of a computer. He adopts a kind of rhythm in thinking, with conscious thought – analysing problems – alternating with unconscious thought, done as if in an unseen workshop where the process of analysing, synthesizing and valuing continue while we get on with other things:

Later, when a new problem arose, I would think it over and, if the answer was not immediately apparent, I would let it go for a while, and it was as if it went the rounds of the brain cells looking for guidance that could be retrieved, for by next morning, when I examined the problem again, more often than not the solution came up right away That judgment seemed to be come to almost unconsciously, and my conviction is that during the time I was not consciously considering the problem, my subconscious had been turning it over and relating it to my memory; it had been held up to the light of the experience I had had in past years, and the way through the difficulties became obvious. ... It is only the rare and most complex problems that require the hard toil of protracted mental effort.

What Thomson describes so well is the continuous process of learning not only to think for himself but to have confidence in his judgment. Yet there is always the danger of overconfidence. The chief symptom is a loss of humble open-mindedness, a growing indifference to the opinions of others well qualified to give their views and advice.

Time is a limited resource for all of us. Leaders at the senior level have to be able to discriminate between those around them – or approaching them – who have something relevant and important to say, and can say it concisely, and those who lack these two credentials. This principle applies to discussion with groups as well as with individuals.

As Osander, the Greek author of *On Generalship* written in the first century CE, implies, there is a golden mean to be found between confidence in your own judgment and being open to the judgments of others, as voiced either collectively or individually:

> The general must be neither so unstable in his judgment that he entirely mistrusts himself, nor so obstinate as to think that nothing that another person has thought up is going to be better than what he himself thinks. Inevitably if a leader heeds everyone else and never himself, he will suffer numerous reverses. On the other hand, if he virtually never listens to others but always only to himself, he will also make many mistakes in consequence.

At the end of the day, however, after the kind of reflection that Thomson outlines, you do have to follow your own judgment. And that is as true in our personal lives as in our place of work. As Montagne says, 'I listen with attention to the judgments of all men; but as far as I can remember, I have followed none but my own.'

* * * * * * *

The two obvious base ingredients of 'reason and calm judgment, the qualities especially belonging to a leader' are *intelligence* and *experience*. Together, the ancient Greeks believed, they equipped the leader not only to take the right decisions but to do so at the right time and in the right way. For the Greek historian Thucydides, the Athenian general and statesman Themistocles is the epitome of this quality, which they called *phronesis*, practical wisdom.

Born into a family of no distinction – a father of low status and an alien mother – as a boy Themistocles showed unusual ability and application. He is living proof of a claim made by Pericles, namely that in Athens 'what counts is not membership of a particular class, but the actual ability which the man possesses'. True to his early promise, Themistocles persuaded the Athenians to develop Piraeus as a port and then to use the income from their rich silver deposits to expand and improve their fleet of warships. Under his generalship, the Athenians won a great naval victory over the Persians at Salamis (480), foundations for growing their wide maritime empire. Thucydides gives us some idea of his multi-faceted talent:

Themistocles was a man who showed an unmistakable natural genius; in this respect he was quite exceptional, and beyond all others deserves our admiration. Without studying a subject in advance or deliberating over it later, but using simply the intelligence that was his by nature, he had the power to reach the right conclusion in matters that have to be settled on the spur of the moment and do not admit of long discussions, and in estimating what was likely to happen, his forecasts of the future were always more reliable than those of others. He would perfectly well explain any subject with which he was familiar, and then outside his own department he was still capable of giving an excellent opinion. He was particularly remarkable at looking into the future and seeing there the hidden possibilities for good or evil. To sum him up in a few words, it may be said that through force of genius and by rapidity of action this man was supreme at doing precisely the right thing at precisely the right moment.

In Aristotle's discussion of ethics, *phronesis* plays a central part. It is essentially the practical judgment as to what to do and how to do it in a morally challenging situation. *Phronesis* is 'imperative', writes Aristotle; 'it gives orders.' The *phroninos* (practically wise person) is a doer with skill and experience. In the Greek gospels, for example, it is the wise man (*phroninos*) who builds his house on rock, whereas his foolish neighbour knows no better than to build on sand. Therefore, when the winter storms come, his house stands and the other one falls.

In Aristotle's writings on ethics the practically wise person, however, is more than just a doer. He or she is a thinker. They employ their practical wisdom to discover what is good for the individual and the community. At the global level of leadership, that means seeking to identify what conduces to the good life as a whole, for both mankind present and to come, and also all the whole of life on our complex and fragile planet.

No one, then, can be practically wise in this broader sense unless he or she is good: for one of the surest signs of a good leader is that they seek to define what is good for their chosen field of work, and also as citizens of the world – for the larger communities of which they are members.

* * * * * * *

Long ago, in the early Middle Ages, an alchemist was working late at night seeking 'the philosopher's stone', the formula that turns common materials into gold. By chance he placed in his crucible intelligence, experience and goodness. In the morning, when he took the crucible off the coals, he found pure gold. He called it *practical wisdom*.

14

What the leader believes and hopes

The only way to lead is to show people the future.
A leader is a dealer in hope.

NAPOLEON

BE, KNOW, DO sums up the conventional wisdom – much as outlined in this book – concerning the essentials of being a leader. Yet there are two other aspects which call for our attention – what the real leader *believes* and *hopes*.

Great conductors believe in the greatness of their orchestras, and that belief arms them to elicit greatness from the musicians involved, both corporately as a team and individually as instrumentalists. The human potential for greatness – if we view humanity as a whole, past and present – is theoretically unlimited, for the human mind is the greatest wonder in the universe. Leaders turn that theory into practice, just as turbines turn rivers into energy.

Another way of looking at the same picture is to turn it upside down and to say that great orchestras deserve great conductors. As the Roman historian Livy once said, 'Rome being great, deserved great leaders.' Not that it always found them. Then, as today, some nations, institutions and organizations have to prove their greatness only by surviving long tenures of poor leadership at their head. As poor leaders are without shame, only time brings any remedy for the damage they can inflict on their fellow citizens. As a Hebrew proverb says, *When God wants to punish the sheep, he sends them a blind shepherd.*

Even deeper than the leader's implicit belief or trust in the greatness of people is their faith in the inalienable goodness of man. For example, Nelson Mandela, reflecting on twenty-eight years as a prisoner on Robben Island, has this to say:

> Even in the grimmest times in prison, when my comrades and I were pushed to our limits, I would see a glimmer of humanity in one of the guards, perhaps just for a second, but that was enough to reassure me and keep me going. Man's goodness is a flame that can be hidden but never extinguished.

Goodness may be understood as a holistic property of a group or a society as a whole, not just the quality of an individual's character. As Aristotle points out:

It's possible that the multitude, though not individually composed of good men, nevertheless in coming together becomes better than its members. Not as individuals but as a whole.

Compare communal dinners, which are better than those supplied out of a single purse. For when there are many, each individual has a portion of virtue and good sense. And when they come together, just as the multitude becomes a single individual with many feet and many hands and possessing many senses, so also it becomes one individual in its moral disposition and intellect.

In a letter to a friend, Pliny the Younger puts it even more succinctly:

In a group there is a certain great collective wisdom. Though its individual members may be deficient in judgment, the group as a whole has much.

Some individuals are – to all intents and purposes – thoroughly evil. Yet Shakespeare reminds us that 'there is some soul of goodness in things evil, would men observingly distil it out'.

Shortfalls of goodness and integrity in some ordinary people – deficiencies of character not personality – mean that those who believe or trust in others will find themselves being let down from time to time. In professional as in personal life, this experience can be painful. It brings with it the temptation to become completely disillusioned about human nature, as if to punish all people for the sins of two or three. But cynics never make good leaders. In fact good persons tend to take a very different line.

'It is happier to be sometimes cheated', said Dr Samuel Johnson, 'than not to trust'. Long ago in ancient China, Lao Tzu came to the same conclusion:

> Those who are good I treat as good. Those who are not good I also treat as good. In so doing I gain in goodness. Those who are of good faith I have faith in. Those who are lacking in good faith I also have faith in. In so doing I gain in good faith.

In other words, they refuse to surrender their goodness on account of those who have treated them or theirs with inhumanity.

At first sight it may seem irrational to trust others as if they are men and women of integrity and honour. But there is an argument that it is a rational policy to adopt. That case is made by a German philosopher called Hans Vaihinger (1852–1933). In his book *The Philosophy of As If*, Vaihinger explored in some depth:

> Notions which *cannot* stand for realities, can be treated *as if* they did, because to do so leads to practical results.

An obvious example is science, where the assumption *as if* truth or understanding order lies beneath the surface of things has led to discovery after discovery. Nobody knows what truth is, and yet, as Pascal says, 'We have an idea of truth, invincible to all scepticism.' But to act *as if* it exists and can be explored and mapped is the belief or faith of a great scientist like Einstein. Seneca, the Roman writer, who prophesied that great scientific discoveries would be made in the centuries after his death, gives today's scientists their charter: 'Truth is open to everyone, and the claims are not all staked yet.'

In other words, trusting others – believing in their integrity or goodness – can be justified on pragmatic grounds: it works.

* * * * * * *

Consider this sentence in Ordway Tead's book *The Art of Leadership* (1935):

The greater leaders have acted *as if* life's values were real and permanent; *as if* living possessed an inner meaning and significance; *as if* the good once attained could not be lost or destroyed; and *as if* courage, endurance and acceptance of the inevitable were worthy adult attributes. (Italics mine)

You can see that Tead is here boldly applying the philosophy of *as if* to life as a whole. 'A man of hope and forward-looking mind', as Wordsworth writes. For here I think that *hope* serves us better than *believe*.

To be *optimistic*, in contrast to pessimistic, usually implies a temperamental confidence that all will turn out for the best. Unlike *hopeful* it often suggests a failure to consider things closely or realistically or, even, a willingness to be guided by illusions rather than facts. To be *hopeful*, on the other hand, implies some ground, and often reasonably good grounds, for one's having hope; it therefore typically suggests confidence in which there is little or no self-deception or which may be the result of a realistic consideration of possibilities.

Hope implies some degree of belief – in the idea that one may expect what one desires or longs for. Although it seldom implies certitude, it usually connotes confidence and often (especially in religious use) implies profound assurance.

No one has proved with any degree of certitude that there is some ulterior purpose or meaning to our human life – some undiscovered ends that give humankind a destiny rather than a fate – and which has the potential of making our individual lives worthwhile.

It is equally true, however, that no one has yet proved with certainty that life does *not* have these values.

You can see now why Napoleon called a leader a 'dealer in hope': for what all leaders tend to do, regardless of their field – or indeed their level – is to create a climate of hope. They do so by themselves, sharing widely their confidence that the end or outcome is going to be favourable or at least for the best. *Hope* is the oxygen of the human spirit, for it is the atmosphere in which men and women can breathe; it breeds a spirit where all want to work together as one, giving their best to the common cause.

The important point is that while hope is still alive you are in with a chance. As Alexander Dubcek, leader of the Czech uprising against the Russians in 1968, said, *'hope dies last; the person who loses hope also loses the sense of his future.'*

Take Dag Hammarskjöld as an example. As secretary general of the United Nations, the second to hold that office, he was the leader in the efforts to maintain peace in a world divided into Western and Eastern blocs. As the vision of a higher form of international society after the trauma of the Second World War, a new order of peace, seemed doomed, Hammarskjöld refused to abandon hope: 'Sometimes that hope – the hope for that kind of reaction – is frustrated', he said, *'but it is a hope which is undying.'*

G. K. Chesterton once said that anyone can hope when things look really hopeful. It is only when everything is hopeless that hope begins to be a strength at all. Like all the spiritual virtues, he added, *'hope is as unreasonable as it is indispensable.'*

That leaves us with a certain freedom to choose. And, as Robert Frost suggests, it is an important choice, especially for a young person standing on the threshold of their adult life.

Looking back with hindsight, you may be aware that at some point – you may never be quite sure when – you *did* make that momentous choice. The unpromising path, the one that you had to travel alone, proved against all the odds to be the right one for you. Robert Frost writes of such an experience in his poem 'The Road Not Taken':

> *I shall be telling this with a sigh*
> *Somewhere ages and ages hence;*
> *Two roads diverged in a wood, and I,*
> *I took the one less travelled by*
> *And that has made all the difference.*

Leaders tend to be among those who choose the positive path rather than the negative one. Or as Teilhard de Chardin expressed it, they deliberately choose the plus rather than the minus. And, it must be added, you are also more likely to find better company on the positive path.

Such beliefs or hopes belong, however – it must be said again – to Vaihinger's broad category of 'notions that which *cannot* stand for realities, but which if treated *as if* they do produce a never-failing store of beneficial or fruitful results'. As you will have guessed, I am firmly in Vaihinger's camp here, but it is just my personal opinion. What do you think?

* * * * * * *

In 1930, thanks to a trust fund set up for the purpose by a local family, the University of St Andrew's in Scotland became the first university in the world to establish a series of annual lectures on leadership. Many famous men delivered these lectures over the next twenty years, but arguably the best was the first one, 'Montrose and Leadership', delivered by John Buchan, novelist and governor general of Canada. In the course of the lecture, he uttered these words, a fitting conclusion for both this chapter and indeed this book as a whole:

> One last word. We may analyse leadership meticulously, like a chemical compound, but we shall never extract its inner essence. There will always be something which escapes us, for in leadership there is a tincture of the miraculous.

> I should define the miraculous element as a response of spirit to spirit. There is in all men, even the basest, some kinship with the divine, something which is capable of rising superior to common passions and the lure of easy rewards, superior to pain and loss, superior even to death. The true leader evokes this. The greatness in him wins a response, an answering greatness in his followers.

> The task of leadership is not to put greatness into humanity, but to elicit it, for the greatness is already there.

Conclusion

There must be a beginning in any great matter,
but the continuing unto the end until it be
thoroughly finished yields the true glory.
SIR FRANCIS DRAKE

OUR HUMAN GREATNESS lies in our ability to transcend ourselves in the service of that which has greater value to us than ourselves. There is not a single man or woman who has not had great moments, who has not risen to rare occasions. It is true that we need situations which call out the best in us as leaders, but all leaders can prepare themselves for such a time. Nor will opportunities be lacking, for as Walt Whitman writes, 'It is provided in the essence of things, that from any fruition of success, no matter what, shall come forth something to make a greater struggle necessary.'

The author Graham Greene was once asked if he considered himself to be a great novelist. 'Not great', he replied, 'but one of the best.' It may be that personal greatness in leadership may elude most leaders, dependent as it is upon situations which evoke it as well as on one's gifts as a leader. But all leaders can and should aspire to being 'one of the best'.

Real excellence goes hand in hand with humility, that unlikely leadership virtue. Humility includes both seeing the truth about oneself and also being open to learning more about good leadership. It suggests, too, that necessary sense of the greatness in others, for 'the task of leadership is not to put greatness into humanity, but to elicit it, for the greatness is there already'.

How far you can progress in that art depends upon your natural ability, your opportunities and your willingness to learn. Why is continuous learning so important? Because it develops your *capability*. Two thousand years ago, Cicero said the same thing. He admitted the power of natural talent, but went on to say, 'When the method and discipline of knowledge are added to talent, the result is usually altogether outstanding.'

By developing your capability you are adding to your resources: the stock or reserve which you can draw on when necessary. Your ability to meet and handle situations is enhanced. In a word, you are becoming a more resourceful person.

You cannot teach leadership; it can only be learnt: This has been often said. True? Well, half-true. But it certainly takes *continuous* learning on your part throughout your career if you are to become 'one of the best'.

The first principle for making headway is to be focused on the role of leader and its functional responsibilities, without worrying about your own particular traits or qualities. If you get your functions right, your qualities will look after themselves. As the Spanish say, *What you do, you become.*

In the Western tradition of leadership, the great British prime minister William Gladstone – you may recall – emphasized the importance of doing just that. So central is the principle he states that it is worth a reminder here:

We are to respect our responsibilities, not ourselves.

We are to respect the duties of which we are capable, not our capabilities simply considered.

There is to be no complacent self-contemplation, ruminating on self.

When the self is viewed, it must always be in the most intimate connexion with its purpose.

For that, indeed, has been the theme of this book. A good part of the journey to becoming an effective strategic leader, I believe, is already behind you once you are clear in your mind what the job entails.

Once you are clear in your mind what others expect from a leader, you can apply yourself with growing confidence to the lifelong task of developing – or acquiring – the knowledge, skills and personal qualities you need to achieve success.

At any level, leadership is a practical art. You learn it by doing it. Really the most that a book like this one can do is to cut down the time that you take to learn by experience. Or, putting it another way, it offers you the opportunity to learn from the experience of others what works and what doesn't work.

To make progress as a leader you need both knowledge of principles – the timeless yet ever timely truths about leadership – and plenty of experience, preferably in more than one field and at more than one level. It is when the sparks jump between principles and practice, theory and experience, that learning takes place. Then you will find yourself continually moving forwards and upwards on the path of leadership.

If this book has aroused in you the desire to be 'one of the best' as a leader, my pen will rest. If, moreover, you have found some practical ideas and suggestions that will take you on our way, I shall be delighted. Beyond that I hope that somewhere you may have heard the music of leadership, for ultimately, as Field Marshal Lord Slim said, 'Leadership is about the spirit.'

If you ever get lost in the ever-expanding library of leadership books, always go back to the Three-Circles model – achieving the task, building the team and developing the individual. However long or short your journey may be it will serve you well as a compass in your pocket – or, better still, as engraved in your mind, so that you don't have to think about it – it is part of who you are.

Lastly, I hope that you will have found some seeds of inspiration in these pages, for if you are inspired as a leader, you will find it within your power to inspire others. Enough from me:

Friend, you have read enough.
If you desire still more,
then be the odyssey yourself,
and all that it stands for.

ANGELUS SILESIUS, SEVENTEENTH-CENTURY
GERMAN POET

INDEX